External Research Associates Program Monograph

D1824336

DELEGITIMIZING AL-QAEDA:
A JIHAD-REALIST APPROACH

Paul Kamolnick

March 2012

*****

Comments pertaining to this report are invited and should be forwarded to: Director, Strategic Studies Institute, U.S. Army War College, 45 Ashburn Drive, Bldg. 47, Carlisle, PA 17013-5046.

*****

This manuscript was funded by the U.S. Army War College External Research Associates Program. Information on this program is available on our website, *www.StrategicStudiesInstitute.army.mil*, at the Opportunities tab.

*****

*****

The Strategic Studies Institute publishes a monthly e-mail newsletter to update the national security community on the research of our analysts, recent and forthcoming publications, and upcoming conferences sponsored by the Institute. Each newsletter also provides a strategic commentary by one of our research analysts. If you are interested in receiving this newsletter, please subscribe on the SSI website at *www.StrategicStudiesInstitute.army.mil/newsletter/*.

ISBN 1-58487-522-4

FOREWORD

During the past 2 decades, America and the world have witnessed the ignoble rise and now-pending destruction of the al-Qaeda terrorist entity, one of the modern world's most vicious and successful transnational organizations. Scholars and national security personnel have dedicated vast resources to dissecting and analyzing al-Qaeda's ideological, strategic, organizational, and tactical strengths and weaknesses. Notable in this entire debate, however, has been the repeated refrain among scholars and U.S. policymakers that we have yet to design and execute a successful messaging campaign that effectively attacks and delegitimizes al-Qaeda in the eyes of potential recruits.

Dr. Paul Kamolnick's monograph is designed to address that present lacuna. It is not in the realm of so-called narrative, ideology, or a "war of ideas," he states, but in the realms of Islamic law, jurisprudence, and U.S. foreign policy that this delegitimizing can and should be waged. First, it is al-Qaeda's violations of the jurisprudence regulating the lawful waging of the military jihad and also its reckless, catastrophic damage to the Islamic cause that most undercuts al-Qaeda's appeal. And second, our willingness to engage in an honest and forthright appraisal of U.S. policies in the Muslim world, coupled with a genuine willingness to address long-simmering grievances, can also significantly undercut al-Qaeda's appeal.

It is incumbent, Kamolnick concludes, for national security decisionmakers to develop the motivation, capability, and sophistication to promulgate and execute a carefully calibrated messaging strategy on these bases. Kamolnick's suggestion that al-Qaeda's mass casualty terrorism violates the Islamic law of war and that the key to dealing with al-Qaeda is a tractable clash of interests and not an intractable clash of civilizations is, if true, a welcome message indeed.

DOUGLAS C. LOVELACE, JR.
Director
Strategic Studies Institute

ABOUT THE AUTHOR

PAUL KAMOLNICK is presently full professor of sociology in the Department of Sociology and Anthropology, East Tennessee State University. He is the sole author of two books, co-editor of one, and has sole-authored several articles, review essays, and reviews for journals including *Sociological Theory, Terrorism and Political Violence, Perspectives in Terrorism*, and *Small Wars Journal*. Dr. Kamolnick teaches courses in social theory, sociology of religion, and the sociology of global terrorism. His present research interests include analyzing mechanisms of terrorist radicalization, deradicalization, and disengagement; and the national security implications of newly-emergent post-autocratic Islamist-influenced Muslim-majority nation-states. Dr. Kamolnick holds a Ph.D. from Florida State University.

SUMMARY

The *9/11 Commission Report* identifies three strategic objectives—decapitation, deradicalization, and hardening homeland security—as key to disrupting, dismantling, and ultimately defeating the al-Qaeda terrorist enterprise. Though the first and third have been notably successful, the second objective has been relatively less so.

Approaches to counter-radicalization that rely on so-called "counterideological" or "counternarrative" approaches miss their mark: they presume ending al-Qaeda's reign of terror requires that Islam as a religious faith delegitimize core Islamic and Islamist tenets, including key planks anchoring religious faith. They also fail to acknowledge and engage the breadth and depth of nonreligiously-motivated opposition to existing U.S. foreign and military policy, especially in the Middle East and the Israel-Palestine conflict. Finally, and most specifically, counternarrative approaches unnecessarily burden this strategic objective by casting a net far too wide and capturing in it a vast Islamic, Islamist, and salafist universe whose adherents are overwhelmingly morally repelled by al-Qaeda's terroristic methods.

Islam is a law-governed religious faith that proscribes and prescribes human conduct. The jihad—the religious prescription to struggle and strive in the path/way of Allah until Allah's word reigns supreme throughout the earth—including its military sense, is despite disavowal in popular piety and much modern moderate Islamic discourse, a binding religious prescription. This presumption of an enduring obligation to wage the military jihad is an essential starting-point in potentially delegitimizing al-Qaeda's reign of terror among adherents for whom shari'a compliance is an essential requirement.

Recent important jurisprudential debates among jihad-realist Islamist militants have produced several conclusions that may be used to delegitimize al-Qaeda's terror as both unlawful and imprudent. The majority of those conclusions arise from recent decades of "prison debates" in Muslim-majority societies over the legality, methods, means, and pragmatics of violent rebellion against their own governments.

These rulings are supplemented by others of vital relevance for undermining al-Qaeda terrorism directed principally against noncombatant civilians living in Muslim-minority societies. Among the latter, the most decisive legal rulings include the following: (1) murder is one of the gravest and forbidden of sins; (2) the impermissibility of targeting Muslims, and non-Muslim civilians, especially women, children, the elderly, scholars, and students of knowledge; (3) the impermissible extension of the principle of *Tartarrus*, or human shields; (4) the impermissibility of treachery, violation of oaths, and pacts of security granted (implicitly, or explicitly) to Muslims in non-Muslim majority societies; (5) jihad is impermissible unless specific capacities, conditions, and circumstances are present; (6) permissibility to wage offensive jihad must be granted by parents and creditors; (7) impermissibility of violating a voluntary oath of unconditional allegiance and obedience (*bay'at*) given to one's recognized ruler; (8) the impermissibility of waging offensive jihad under present conditions of Muslim weakness vis-à-vis the infidel powers; (9) the permissibility of jihad, emigration, or a truce when facing infidel occupation; (10) the impermissibility of attacking American civilians of an occupying country in the name of jihad or under its banner; and, (11) the imprudence of al-Qaeda based and inspired terrorism.

It is suggested that relevant policymakers give due regard to the key role that jihad-realist jurisprudential debates hold for contributing to the tactical implosion and marginalization of al-Qaeda's terrorism. Those charged with strategic communication, public diplomacy, and counterterrorist messaging should develop the motivation, capacity, and sophistication to systematically analyze how jihad-realism and a jurisprudence of jihad, may be leveraged for, and not against, vital U.S. national security interests.

Owing to present hostility directed in many quarters against U.S. policies in the Middle East and Muslim world generally, and the Israel-Palestine conflict in particular, however, it is extremely *inadvisable* for the United States to openly promote or publicize any of these initiatives. A key, indeed essential, ingredient for the authority of these findings is that they are viewed as absolutely untainted by any interest, factor, force, or power; rather, these debates rest on the legitimacy of the shari'a and involve credentialed actors of immense stature and learning.

It *is* advisable that the United States do everything within its power to make the case to the Muslim-majority countries, and the Muslim-minority populations in the Muslim diaspora, that as a country we are on the side of the lawful and the just, and we actively seek and promote solutions to long-simmering policy grievances. Our ability as a nation to openly associate with any efforts by internal Muslim actors must be deferred until the perception of our motivations is altered, and altered fundamentally. No amount of spin or messaging matters when daily life and its commonsense interpretation contradict official pretensions and pronouncements.

DELEGITIMIZING AL-QAEDA: A JIHAD-REALIST APPROACH

HOW AL-QAEDA ENDS

Disrupting, dismantling, and eventually defeating al-Qaeda based and inspired transnational terrorism is the declared policy of the U.S. Government.[1] The *9/11 Commission Report* makes reference to three over-arching strategies for defeating this enemy:[2] attacking the al-Qaeda terrorist organization; preventing further radicalization and recruitment to al-Qaeda; and protecting the homeland from future attack.[3]

Evidence strongly suggests that decapitating al-Qaeda[4] and hardening homeland security[5] are having significant strategic effects.[6] Far less success is claimed, however, for the prevention of radicalization and recruitment to al-Qaeda's transnational terrorist campaign. This monograph supplies a distinct approach for partially accomplishing this elusive strategic objective.

It is important to note at the outset that preventing replenishment via incitement, radicalization, and recruitment to the al-Qaeda organization is only one of many factors associated with the certain decline and demise of terrorist campaigns, al-Qaeda included. Briefly, six variables individually or in some combination are predictors of terrorist organizational demise: decapitation, negotiations, success, reorientation, repression, and failure.[7]

Decapitation, along with hardened homeland security measures, has dramatically affected al-Qaeda's capacity for launching its unique "brand" of violent extremism: complex, simultaneous, multiple-target, mass casualty terrorist attacks directed at the U.S.

homeland.[8] Short of a complete revolutionary reorganization of the global international order, al-Qaeda's maximalist global violent extremist ambitions cannot *succeed*. Al-Qaeda's global revolutionary terrorism also rules out *negotiations*; although a deliberate and sustained U.S. strategy of disaggregating al-Qaeda's terrorist network suggests targeting select regional affiliates and associates for whom less ambitious political achievements (e.g., local, national, or specific policy grievance-based) are original drivers.[9] Selective *reorientation* of al-Qaeda from disciplined global mass-casualty violent extremist terrorism toward opportunist criminality and less-ambitious Islamist militancy has occurred, though on a relatively minor scale.[10] *Repression* for our purposes is captured by the above discussion of decapitating the terrorist organization but is somewhat broader and encompasses attacking the organizational capacities of al-Qaeda to persist as an organized terrorist entity.[11]

While the above five correlates contribute in varying degrees to al-Qaeda's dramatically-weakening present capacities, it is the sixth predictor—i.e., *failure*—that is the primary concern of this monograph. This is so because it most directly touches on that heretofore underaccomplished strategic objective noted in the *9/11 Commission Report*: preventing radicalization and recruitment to al-Qaeda's transnational terrorist campaign. Again, it is the intention of this monograph to contribute to that strategic objective vital to declared national policy through the calculated exploitation of failure as a known predictor of terrorist organizational decline and demise.

What is meant by terrorist failure as applied to al-Qaeda? Failure here refers to a two-dimensional nightmare scenario facing the al-Qaeda terrorist enterprise:

internal *implosion* and external *marginalization*. Indeed, these combined dimensions account for a significant swath of variance explained in terrorist failure: "Most terrorism ends," Audrey K. Cronin claims:

> because the group employing the tactic fails and eventually disintegrates. The short life-span and limited success of most groups that use terrorism demonstrate that violence deliberately targeted against civilians repels rather than attracts popular support. Indiscriminate killing creates a backlash and undermines political staying power. Terrorism creates havoc, murders innocent people, draws morbid fascination; but it is insufficient to achieve political or social change.[12]

Evidence drawn from previous terrorist campaigns indicates four pathways to internal implosion: (1) the failure to attract new generations of membership and leadership; (2) in-fighting and fractionalization; (3) loss of operational control;[13] and, (4) offering exit ramps for marginal members seeking to separate from the organization.[14] "Implosion," Cronin states, "happens when there is in-fighting over the mission, operations, competition for dominance,[15] differences of ideology, loss of interest among members—even simple exhaustion or burnout."[16]

Marginalization, on the other hand, signifies organizational isolation and distance from a broader mass of actual or potential supporters. "Groups that do not implode," she continues, "may be cut off from their supporters. Marginalization occurs when there is a diminution of active or passive support, or even a popular backlash against the violence."[17]

From the above one may predict that terrorist groups end *because* they are terrorist groups. As a type of political violence—excepting those terrorists that abandon terrorist means, reconnect to a broader mass, and transform into a legitimate insurgent or political entity — sustenance must become ever more perilous and fraught with all-too-human imperfections. As extremist outliers, they are isolated within, and therefore simultaneously inhabit the remotest outskirts and fringes of an imagined ideal, cause, or community they arrogantly presume to lead as vanguard. Further, they are marginalized by moral revulsion owing to the killing of innocents and the cold logic of a ruthless killing machine that lacks a pragmatic, hopeful, believable Other realizable by real persons in real time.[18]

A JIHAD-REALIST JURISPRUDENTIAL APPROACH

However distasteful to U.S. national security decisionmakers, the presumption of Islamic supremacism and a past-perfect Islamic utopian "golden age" in contrast to an age of pagan ignorance and infidelity; belief in the exclusive right of the Islamic call and right to rule all of humankind; extremely-negative caricatures of certain features of present-day Western societies; and vehement opposition to U.S. foreign policy in the Middle East (and in particular what is regarded as a hypocritical embrace of democracy, support for autocracy, and one-sided support for Israeli occupation) is professed by many observant and "non-jihadi" Muslims. On pragmatic grounds alone, therefore, it is inadvisable to presume that destroying al-Qaeda based and inspired terrorism necessitates displacing Islamic supremacism and its essentially apologetic "narrative."[19] Moreover, though the majority of observant Muslims in daily popular piety disavows the religious prescription to wage military

4

jihad, the legal case upholding an enduring obligation to call others to Islam (*da'wa*); to wage the military jihad until the entire world proclaims the word of Allah supreme; and to enjoy the most privileged status and fruits awaiting a true *mujahid* in paradise, is, in fact, a compelling one.[20] Neither popular piety, moderates, liberals, or modernists have to date, in the opinion of the present author, successfully refuted it.[21]

In this monograph, a jihad-realist jurisprudential approach is operationalized as a tactical contribution to the imploding of al-Qaeda.[22] This approach is potentially of greater yield, however, since unlike those traditional categories of terrorist littering the political violence landscape (e.g., separatist, ethno-nationalist, communist, anarchist, or doomsday cults), al-Qaeda legitimizes its self-proclaimed right to wage jihad based on what it claims is a faithful adherence to Islamic law.

Islam is a strictly-monotheistic, law-centered, world religion. Its legal and moral principles are rooted in a revealed sacred scripture (*Qur'an*), traditional accounts of Prophet Muhammad's life (*Ahadith*), and nearly 1,400 years of jurisprudential tradition. Aptly described as aspiring toward a universal divine nomocracy,[23] all persons regardless of social status, class, race, sex, tribe, or family background are duty-bound to strive for righteous intention and conduct in daily life. In its orthodox Sunnite and Shi'ite forms, Islam is quintessentially a religion commanding lawful and forbidding lawless behavior.[24] Islamic law also prescribes a law of warfare, and for observant Muslims, the military jihad is a binding religious prescription.[25]

There is no attempt in this monograph to deny, minimize, or otherwise obfuscate this martial religious prescription. In the opinion of this author, a genuinely

effective means for tactically imploding and marginal-
izing al-Qaeda — particularly in the eyes of those deeply religiously-motivated potential recruits for whom
religious law is a *sine qua non* for participation — *must*
presume the validity of Islamically-prescribed military jihad, and *in those terms*, objectively assess and de-
cisively refute the validity of al-Qaeda's declaration of
war and subsequent global terrorist campaign.[26] This
approach proposed by the present author is designed
to target exactly the type of person to which Noman
Benotman, former Libyan Islamic Fighting Group violent militant "jihadist" refers, when he states that for
genuine dialogue to even begin, "The starting point
has to be that jihad is legitimate, otherwise no one will
listen."[27] Three essential additional premises must also
be conceded if an Islamically-rooted legal case against
al-Qaeda's reign of terror is to be valid, namely first,
that there is an absolute legal distinction between "legitimate jihad and terrorism";[28] second, that terrorism
is *"haram"* (forbidden);[29] and third, in addition to being forbidden, "grave Sharia violations"[30] have accompanied terrorist methodologies.[31]

WAGING JIHAD: AL-QAEDA'S VIOLATIONS OF THE SHARI'A[32]

A summary of select jihad-realist jurisprudential objections raised against al-Qaeda based and inspired terrorism is provided.[33] Before embarking on
this task, however, it is crucial to understand that for
those young seekers of truth and justice targeted by
al-Qaeda's tactical propaganda, taking jihad "off the
table" means potentially leaving on the table a mas-
sive structure of injustice that still demands a remedy
in their eyes. If not jihad, then what? If terrorism is

indeed impermissible, how then are Muslims to fight back? Consider the following three online posts in response to the republication of a letter[34] by prominent salafi Saudi Sheikh Salman al-Oudah, calling for a categorical condemnation of terrorism, regardless of motive or cause, without hesitation, "ifs," "ands," or "buts."[35] These were just three of 185 posts over a 4-day period from al-Qaeda sympathizers (a distinct minority) to modern, justice-seeking, young westernized Muslims (the vast majority)—all convinced the Muslim world requires definite action in its defense.

> **Naeem**: Very nice article [Sheikh Oudah's] and follow-up comments [three other Sheikhs]. I like how it's been made unequivocally clear what Jihad IS NOT. However, I'm convinced that we must simultaneously make clear what Jihad IS. Otherwise, confusion will persist. This article, while condemning the ill-advised actions and beliefs of many disenfranchised youth, does not allay their worries and concerns. The frustrations are still there and are VERY REAL. Should we cease to be concerned about the oppressions [sic] facing the Muslim Ummah? If not, what avenues do we have open to us? If (combative) Jihad is one of them, then what type of Jihad-oriented activities and efforts should we be supporting? In what manner? It is incumbent upon our scholars to not only teach us what is deplorable, but what is commendable, particularly in this very gray area of 21st century Jihad.[36]

> **Yaser**: Absolutely valid concern [raised by Naeem], and I believe it is the right of every Muslim, especially those in the west, to know what is the right and valid way of Jihad, away from any zealous spirit or apologetic approach. I hope we can fulfill this request in future posts and articles insha'Allah [God willing].[37]

Mystrugglewithin: Naeem's comment, and your [Yaser] feedback summarize everything that most of us here are concerned with.[38]

It is clear that al-Qaeda's "center of gravity" is a younger generation of savvy, justice-seeking recruits and, owing to this, that prominent *shaykhs* and *ulema* are attempting to argue that, yes, justice is supreme, but unjust means can never attain just ends. It is entry to Paradise itself that will be denied to those using sinful or criminal shortcuts — even if those actions are based in ignorance of one's religion — and discounting genuine human costs. Shaykh al-Oudah clarifies these very consequences and the choice of two paths awaiting these youth.

> The merciful thing to do is to tell those young people who have been deceived, and *those who are set to join their ranks tomorrow,* that: 'This path you are taking is not going to bring you to your goal. It will not save you from Hell or earn you Paradise. Whoever wants success in this life, salvation in the next, and Allah's pleasure should adhere to the true teachings of Islam and keep far away from bloodshed and strife. Do not attempt to reinterpret the faith so as to justify acts that are clearly and patently evil. In the boldness with which you commit mortal sins, you engage in crimes far worse in Allah's estimation than those whom you purport to condemn (italics added).'[39]

Sayyid al-Imam Abd-al-Aziz al-Sharif (aka Dr. Fadl), imprisoned former senior shari'a scholar for the Egyptian Jihad Organization and al-Qaeda's former shari'a guide — whose guidelines for legal jihad we shall soon consider — also understands this center of gravity all too well. It is not difficult to read between these lines. To the question posed by *Al-Hayah* journalist Muhammad Salah, "What advice would you give Muslim youths regarding jihad?" he replies:

> You should know that jihad is right, but beware those who exploit the youths' ignorance of their religion and their zeal for Islam, pushing them to engage in jihad for which the means and resources are not available. They end up in jails or getting uselessly killed. This allows those who trade in Muslim youths' zeal to earn reputation and donations. You must know that jihad has conditions and impediments, which must be carefully considered. The reasons for jihad in and of themselves are not sufficient to go to jihad, such as the presence of the enemy [in Muslim lands]. You should consider whose interest the jihad will serve. The Prophet, may God's peace and prayers be upon him, said: 'He who fights to elevate God's word follows God's path.' This is an agreed upon Hadith. Do not leave your country and travel for jihad without permission from your Muslim parents. Do not move to a place without a full knowledge of circumstances.[40]

And in the same interview, in response to Muhammad Salah quoting Egyptian radical fundamentalist and al-Qaeda member Muhammad Khalil al-Hakayimah who "on 26 September . . . said: 'Young Muslims will only trust the fatwas of the shaykhs and ulema who advocate jihad'," Sayyid Imam retorts:

> O Al-Hakayimah: When God Almighty said: 'O Messenger, rouse the Believers to the fight' [Koranic verse, Al-Anfal 8:65], He ordered him to begin with himself. God Almighty says: 'Then fight in Allah's cause — Thou art responsible only for thyself — and rouse the believers' [Koranic verse, An-Nisa 4:84]. The Messenger is a good example for us, for he led his companions in fighting. *Quit the remote control electronic jihad,* and come to set a good example for the people here, espe-

cially because you deny being powerless. Otherwise, *your victims who are recruited on the internet* will purposelessly fill prisons, just because they believed you, unaware of the rule: 'If you are my imam, you should stand in front of me in battle (italics added).'[41]

And even more emphatically, Sayyid Imam states:

My document ['Rationalization'] *will also save many Muslim young men from being lured by al-Qaeda over Internet and being taught treachery and betrayal.* It will save many of al-Qaeda's current followers and admirers who will hasten to repent before they are betrayed and encouraged to be treacherous to others, something for which they would be punished on the Day of Judgment. This document has caused some people to be released from jail and brought back happiness to many homes that had been living in sorrow. If the Muslims' enemies profit from this, this is incidental and not the result of agreement just as they benefited from our participation in the Afghan jihad. Yet the Muslim people's benefit is greater. Not everything that benefits the enemy is to be disdained (italics added).[42]

Let us now consider the principal Islamic shari'a objections to al-Qaeda based and inspired terrorism. We also briefly consider jurisprudential objections identified in this same literature that may ultimately prove more persuasive to potential recruits unmoved by strict compliance with often scholastically encumbered jurisprudential disputes, who seek concrete results manifest in tangible evidence of Muslim empowerment, well-being, and the expansion of the Islamic call.

It is beyond the scope of the present monograph, and the competency of the present author, to enter into a detailed consideration of the entire chain of reasoning and jurisprudential proofs offered for each point listed below. Genuine shari'a scholars are required to glean from every issue they consider some combination of reliance on the primary sources — Qur'an, Hadith, ijma, and qiyas — to derive valid legal opinions. The unrivaled source of authority in each dispute, barring corruption or circumvention of this process, is both the scholarly and jihadi reputation of the participants to this debate, and their ultimate ability to prevail in the ongoing worldwide conversation about the jihad imperative in the 21st century. Especially key is the fact that these disputant scholars are unconditionally associated with the religious duty to wage jihad, and are untainted by any conflicts of interest, for example, service on behalf of regimes perceived to be self-serving who seek to undermine violent rebellion not on grounds of religion, but sheer regime survival.[43]

These objections considered in their entirety amount to violations of what is in essence an Islamic law of armed conflict, including the right and duty to violent rebellion against an unjust ruler. These objections overlap, but naturally fall into two distinct clusters. The first concern predominantly Muslim societies in which violent armed Islamist organizations wage what they claim is jihad against what they assert are "apostate" regimes (i.e., declarations of "takfir of the ruler" or regime). The rules governing jihad, declaring one an apostate, and the many issues arising from targeting various kinds of person, are addressed here.

The second cluster comprises those objections of greatest interest to those non-Muslim majority societies, including the United States, targeted by al-Qaeda's reign of terror. Though some overlap exists with the first cluster, unique legal issues are raised, and shari'a violations identified. It is this second cluster that is of greatest interest to citizens living in predominantly non-Muslim societies presently targeted by al-Qaeda.

The Jihad-Realist Rejection of Violent Rebellion and Takfir.[44]

The following shari'a violations have been most consistently cited by an emergent consensus of jihad-realist militant Islamists who have religiously delegitimized violent armed conflict directed against their governments.

1. *The Impermissible Rejection of Scholarly Authority.* This includes the failure to recognize the legitimate authority of learned Islamic experts and scholars on matters pertaining to shari'a, its legitimate methodology, and as a corollary, the need for deep skepticism about persons whose scholarly credentials in shari'a are insufficient, particularly in such weighty matters as inflicting harm and violence on others.[45]

2. *The Impermissibility of Extremism and Fanaticism.* Fanaticism, extremism, and immoderation violate explicit and unambiguous Islamic tenets and traditions. Immoderation is the gateway to violations of the shari'a, and most often results in undermining the interests and values of the Umma.[46]

3. *Murdering Muslims is Haram.* Unlawfully murdering Muslims is an absolute sin whose moral gravity is second only to the denial of the singularity and sovereignty of Allah.[47]

4. *The Impermissible Declarations of Takfir.* The impermissibility of *takfir* — declaring another Muslim an apostate and therefore rendering their lives and property forfeit — stressing especially its historic consequence in undermining social solidarity, sowing

12

chaos, creating disorder, facilitating dissension (fit-nah), and unleashing mayhem.[48]

5. *The Impermissibility of Violating the Lives, Property, and Honor of Non-Muslims Granted Promises of Security.* An extensive jurisprudential literature exists regulating the permissible security granted non-Muslims visiting or residing in Muslim lands. It is impermissible to target civilians involved in leisure, tourism, business, or other affairs.[49]

6. *The Religiously Ignorant, Impermissible, and Pragmatically Disastrous Isolation of Jihad as a Means of Promoting Allah's Word.*[50] This jihadism is characterized by unlawful, inadvisable risk-taking in matters of military action, eschewing for example, legal and customary requirements bearing on such factors as the relative strength of one's opponents; the relative capacity to wage jihad; the relative availability of less-costly options (i.e., *da'wa*, enforcing the good and forbidding evil, isolation, emigration, etc.),[51] and the relative costs to the Umma. This imprudence is likely owing to fanaticism, extremism, and the placing of means before ends, each of which are rooted in religious ignorance or worldly desires. The inflicting of overwhelmingly burdensome costs has not only destroyed lives, property, homes, and families in the short-run, but has also come at the expense of the longer-term benefits, values and abiding interests of the Umma.[52]

7. *Impermissibility of Rejecting the Modern State's Prerogative to Exercise Political Authority and Wage Jihad.* The medieval circumstances dividing the world into Islamic (*Dar al-Islam*) and non-Islamic (*Dar al-Harb*; literally "Abode" or "House" of War) spheres, and elevating the role of Caliph and Caliphate, no longer exists. Collective Muslim majorities are now territorially organized into sovereign nation-states, and the state is

a political organ possessing a legitimate monopoly on the means and use of violence. If today jihad is to be declared and waged to discharge the lawful collective duty (*fard kifaya*) to conduct offensive jihad to expand the Umma, it can only be declared by a legitimate sovereign on the basis of the shari'a.[53]

8. *Impermissible Extremism in the Exercise of the Right to Retribution (the "principle of justice")*. Recall that the range of legal/moral permissibility for a given action is five-fold: absolutely required or commanded (*fard*); commendable or recommended, but not required (*mustahabb*); indifferent, neutral, permissible (*mubah*); discouraged or reprehensible, but not forbidden (*makruh*); absolutely and explicitly forbidden because both sinful and criminal (*haram*). Not only does Islam maintain that charity, mercy, and forgiveness are even greater virtues than mere retribution[54] — though that is certainly just and does restore a lawful reciprocity — permissible conduct (i.e., retribution) has been replaced with terroristic conduct that is forbidden (*haram*).[55]

9. *The General Impermissibility of Violent Rebellion Against a Ruler, and its Necessary Conditions Specified.*[56] It is only under the most dire circumstances that the Muslim community would not be threatened in their lives, security, honor, and possessions by overthrowing a ruler. Apostasy amounting to active disavowal of the Islamic creed and assisting the enemies of the Umma, are today the only sufficient grounds.

The Jihad-Realist Rejection of al-Qaeda Based and Inspired Terrorism.[57]

The above legal rulings apply most specifically to Muslim-majority societies that over past decades have faced violent Islamist rebellions in the name of jihad.

These rulings may be complemented with additional ones of direct and vital relevance, undermining al-Qaeda's reign of terror principally directed against noncombatant civilians living in Muslim-minority societies. The force of these legal objections does not lie in any kind of sentimentalism, but in a deeply-embedded set of principles that legally regulate the military jihad. It is worth restating at the outset, before considering al-Qaeda's chief violations, what a jihad-realist jurisprudential approach is. Such an approach is succinctly stated by Sayyid Imam himself:

> . . . [J]ihad is a continuing religious duty in the Nation of the Muslims, since Allah the Almighty ordained it and until the last one of them combats the imposter together with the Lord Christ [sic][58] peace upon him, at the end of time, as our Prophet Muhammad Allah's prayers and peace upon him told us. The prophet described jihad as "the peak of Islam's hump," for Allah preserves for the Muslims and their religion and their world, their pride and dignity here and in the Hereafter. Thus it is necessary to rationalize the understanding of the religious duty of jihad.[59]

What, then, are the cardinal shari'a objections raised against al-Qaeda based and inspired terrorism?

1. *The Murder of Persons is Haram.* Due to the sacred nature of all life — its absolute sanctity — persons must be secure in their lives, persons, property, possessions, and honor.[60]

2. *The Impermissibility of Targetting Muslims; and non-Muslim Civilians, Especially Women, Children, the Elderly, Scholars and Students of Knowledge.*[61] This is self-explanatory but bears repeating, since it is stated explicitly within the context of non-Muslim majority societies.

3. *The Impermissible Extension of the Principle of Tartarrus* (targeting human shields).[62] The sanctity of life, and specific conditions that must be met for jihad to be waged, almost always render impermissible the killing of a Muslim, even if unintentionally. The jurisprudence of justification has, however, violated these conditions in order to facilitate its unlawful terrorist activities.

4. *The Impermissibility of Treachery, Violation of Oaths and Pacts of Security Granted (implicitly, or explicitly) to Muslims in Non-Muslim Majority societies.*[63] The question of safe passage for non-Muslims in Muslim-majority societies was examined above. This deals with the security pact that governs the duty of Muslims who are provided the opportunity to enter, be secure in, and enjoy the liberties of life, property, possessions, and honor, in a non-Muslim society.

5. *The Impermissibility of Killing on the Basis of Nationality.* There is no precedent in Islam for killing persons on the basis of national affiliation. Since in the modern era Muslims may, and often likely will be, living in non-Muslim societies, this invites the potential killing of Muslims. However, its impermissibility rests on a broader religious tradition that, while distinguishing persons on the basis of faith, does not do so on the basis of territorial residency or citizenship. Osama bin Laden's and Ayman al-Zawahiri's claim that they are targeting "Crusaders" in the "Crusader-Zionist" alliance is shown to be another instance of the jurisprudence of justification.[64]

6. *Jihad is Impermissible Unless Specific Conditions and Capacities are Present.* Jihad is an enduring religious obligation. However, because of the seriousness of such a declaration — the equivalent of a declaration of war, in the West — waging jihad is only permissible if one

16

has taken explicit and careful account of the abilities, circumstances, conditions, and costs involved (relative to perceived benefits, and perceived alternative courses of action) that this religious prescription demands.[65]

7. *Permissibility to Wage Offensive Jihad Must Be Granted by Parents and Creditors.* Individuals participating in an offensive jihad must have these permissions. Persons participating in a defensive jihad, however, generally do not. The costs of abandoning one's parents, families, properties, and possessions, however, must be factored in, and the *ulema* have issued divided opinions. [66]

8. *Impermissibility of Violating a Voluntary Oath of Unconditional Allegiance (bay'at) Given to One's Recognized Ruler.* Osama bin Laden knowingly and willfully disobeyed then supreme leader of the Taliban regime, Mullah Omar, by provoking in word and deed the United States, and thus increasing the likelihood that Afghanistan would be invaded and a Muslim government overthrown. Osama bin Laden was an invited guest enjoying complete security of person, property, and liberty of action. His impermissible actions are widely viewed as the proximate cause of the removal of the Taliban from power, and the calamitous consequences that have resulted from those events.[67]

9. *The Impermissibility of Waging Offensive Jihad Under Present Conditions of Muslim Weakness vis-à-vis the Infidel Powers.* Jihad-realism is not a suicide pact, and the present power imbalance between Muslim and non-Muslim parties recommends against violent means. Other alternatives are available to Muslims "short of war" for advancing the Muslim cause. Until objective conditions favoring military action exist, these alternatives are both permissible and desirable.[68]

10. *The Permissibility of Jihad, Emigration, or a Truce, When Facing Infidel Occupation.* A defensive jihad is understood to be an individual duty (*fard 'ayn*) that devolves on every believer. However, it may be that the costs of such a jihad outweigh the benefits, and other courses of action are legally permissible.[69]

11. *The Impermissibility of Attacking Civilians of an Occupying Country in the Name of Jihad or Under Its Banner.* This is the central legal question of greatest interest to Americans and American policymakers. Regardless of whether a country is presumed to be an occupying country, in this case the presumption by al-Qaeda that the United States is "occupying Muslim lands," it is impermissible to harm civilians or combatants in that home country.[70]

12. *The Imprudence of al-Qaeda Based and Inspired Terrorism.* Behind virtually every legal discussion above is the implicit relation between law and life. Law that does not support life does not last. Religious principles that are radically at odds with the reality principle — the conditions of the world as they exist in reality, not in fantasy or wish-projection — either reinterpret these principles, reform them, or become of mere antiquarian interest. A pragmatic, prudential substrate exists in Islam, as in every other great faith, that relates desired ends to available means, and evaluates courses of action in relation to the actual benefits that arise for its intended beneficiaries. It is on these grounds that the events occurring on September 11, 2001 (9/11) are arguably the most calamitous, catastrophic blow against Islam. A Muslim who is deeply observant, but also wisely pragmatic may then ask: How has Osama Bin Laden's so-called jihad benefitted Islam? What has been the cost to Islam and Muslims worldwide of al-Qaeda's unilateral decision to declare, launch,

and wage a reign of terror whose principal victims are noncombatant civilians, Muslim and non-Muslim? The answer is not hard to find. The mind of the world is not focused on Islam as a majestic, deeply law-abiding, religion of peace, mercy, and justice; but on a religion whose reputation has now been perverted by its association with intolerance, fanaticism, and terror. Bin Laden's gift has not been to expand the sphere of those prepared to hear and respond to the Muslim call but those prepared — by the ignominy of 9/11, and religious ignorance in the West regarding Islam's actual moral soul — to resist it, and indeed extinguish it.[71]

CONCLUSION AND POLICY IMPLICATIONS

Conclusion.

1. Several variables affect the demise and eventual destruction of terrorist organizations. The tactical implosion and marginalization of al-Qaeda based and inspired terrorism is a necessary but insufficient condition for ending al-Qaeda.

2. The *9/11 Report* identifies three key strategic objectives — decapitation, de-radicalization, and homeland security/resilience — as keys to defeating al-Qaeda, and while the first and third have been notably successful, the second objective has been relatively less so.

3. Approaches to counterradicalization that rely on so-called counterideological or counternarrative approaches miss their mark: they presume ending al-Qaeda's reign of terror requires that Islam as a religious faith delegitimize core Islamic and Islamist tenets, including key planks anchoring religious faith, including a Past-Perfect, Present-Imperfect, and Future-

to-be-Perfect belief system that demands the right and duty to make Allah's word Supreme; they fail to acknowledge and engage the breadth and depth of nonreligiously motivated opposition to existing U.S. foreign and military policy, especially in the Middle East and the Israel-Palestine conflict; and most specifically, counternarrative approaches unnecessarily burden this tactical objective by casting their net far too wide and capturing a vast Islamic, Islamist, and *salafist* universe whose adherents are overwhelmingly morally repelled by al-Qaeda's reign of terror.

4. Islam is a law-centered religious faith that proscribes and prescribes human conduct. The jihad—the religious prescription to struggle and strive in the path/way of Allah until Allah's word reigns supreme throughout the earth—including its military sense is, despite disavowal in popular piety and much modern moderate Islamic discourse, a binding religious prescription. This presumption is an essential starting-point in potentially delegitimizing al-Qaeda's reign of terror among adherents for whom shari'a compliance is an essential requirement to wage lawful jihad.

5. Recent important jurisprudential debates among jihad-realist Islamist militants have produced several conclusions that may be used to delegitimize al-Qaeda's reign of terror as both unlawful, and imprudent. The majority of those conclusions arise from recent decades of prison debates in Muslim-majority societies over the legality, methods, means, and pragmatics of violent rebellion against existing governments in Muslim-majority societies. Among the most important shari'a violations are: (1) The impermissible rejection of scholarly authority; (2) The impermissibility of extremism and fanaticism; (3) Murdering Muslims is *haram;* (4) The impermissible declarations of takfir;

(5) The impermissibility of violating the lives, property, and honor of non-Muslims granted promises of security; (6) The religiously ignorant, impermissible, and pragmatically disastrous isolation of jihad as a means of promoting Allah's word; (7) Impermissibility of rejecting the modern state's prerogative to exercise political authority and wage jihad; (8) Impermissible extremism in the exercise of the right to retribution (the "principle of justice"); and, (9) The general impermissibility of violent rebellion against a ruler, and its necessary conditions specified.

6. These rulings may be complimented with additional ones of direct and vital relevance, undermining al-Qaeda's reign of terror directed principally against noncombatant civilians living in Muslim-minority societies. Among the latter, the most decisive legal objections include: (1) The murder of persons is *haram*; (2) The impermissibility of targeting Muslims, and non-Muslim civilians, especially women, children, the elderly, scholars, and students of knowledge; (3) The impermissible extension of the principle of *Tartarrus*; (4) The impermissibility of treachery, violation of oaths, and pacts of security granted (implicitly, or explicitly) to Muslims in non-Muslim majority societies; (5) Jihad is impermissible unless specific capacities, conditions, and circumstances, are present; (6) Permissibility to wage offensive jihad must be granted by parents and creditors; (7) Impermissibility of violating a voluntary oath of unconditional allegiance and obedience (*bay'at*) given to one's recognized ruler; (8) The impermissibility of waging offensive jihad under present conditions of Muslim weakness vis-à-vis the infidel powers; (9) The permissibility of jihad, emigration, or a truce, when facing infidel occupation; (10) The impermissibility of attacking American civilians

of an occupying country in the name of jihad or under its banner; and, (11) The imprudence of al-Qaeda based and inspired terrorism.

Policy Suggestions.

1. Give due regard to the key role that jihad-realist jurisprudential debates hold for contributing to the tactical implosion and marginalization of al-Qaeda's reign of terror.

2. Owing to present hostility directed in many quarters against U.S. policies in the Middle East and Muslim world generally, and the Israel-Palestine conflict in particular, it is extremely *inadvisable* for the United States to openly promote or publicize any of these initiatives. A key, indeed essential, ingredient for the authority of these findings is that they are viewed as absolutely untainted by any interest, factor, force, or power; rather, these debates rest on the legitimacy of the shari'a and involve credentialed actors of immense stature and learning.

3. Those charged with strategic communication, public diplomacy, and messaging generally to promote United States interests should develop the sophistication, capacities, and motivation, to systematically analyze how jihad-realism and a jurisprudence of jihad, may be leveraged for, and not against, these interests.

4. The proper counternarrative frame is not "genuine peaceful pro-Western mainstream Muslim seeking liberal democratic freedoms versus jihadist violent killer seeking the destruction of Western civilization." While relevant to some targets—those for whom Western cultural modernity is a value, and the shari'a of customary or merely historic interest—this coun-

ternarrative is *not* the one to defeat the religiously learned for whom living and dying to promote the word of Allah as supreme, *is* Islam. The debate is one within militant Islamism over the lawfulness of al-Qaeda's methods. It is about whether terrorism is *haram*, and has done virtually incalculable damage to Islam's global image; or it is *fard*, and an essential condition of being a True Mujahid and advancing the Muslim Umma. In this battle it is, ironically, the learned, jihad-realist jurisprudents — lovers of religious truth, and religious law — whose spirit most resembles that of our own learned constitutional scholars. It is the law that they love first, because law is a condition of life; of security; of any reasonable attempt to fashion a lasting and just social order. Impatience and imprudence have always been enemies of the law. It is in essence the law's revenge that is finally wreaking havoc, along with those several other causes, on al-Qaeda's reign of terror.

It is *advisable* that the United States do everything within its power to make the case to the Muslim-majority countries, and the Muslim-minority populations in the Muslim diaspora, that as a country we are on the side of the lawful and the just, and that we actively seek and promote solutions to long-simmering policy grievances. Our ability as a nation to openly associate with any efforts by internal Muslim actors will only be the kiss of death until the perception of our motivations is altered, and altered fundamentally. No amount of spin or messaging matters when daily life and its common-sense interpretation contradicts official pretensions and pronouncements. One should always remember that the "Planes Operation" — the momentous event that shook the world and created an alternative one rooted in war-footing and a threatened "clash of civilizations" was the work of terrorist entrepreneurs whose primary goal was to cause as much pain to the United States as possible, *not* because of its lack of shari'a compliance; *or* its infidelity; *or* its craven and immoral ways; *or* its freedoms. But quite the opposite, for it was seen—certainly through a mindset rooted in paranoia, scapegoating, and a reverse-demonology—as being the singular superpower actor whose support for its ally Israel was the essential condition preventing a resolution of an enduring conflict thousands of miles from its borders—not shari'a, but retribution; not jihad, but terrorism; not Muslim holy war, but terrorist moral rage.[72]

ENDNOTES

1. *National Security Strategy*, Washington, DC: The White House, Office of the President, May 2010, pp. 4, 19-22, available from *www.whitehouse.gov/sites/default/files/rss_viewer?national_security? strategy.pdf*; *National Strategy for Countering Terrorism*, Washington, DC: The White House, Office of the President, June 2011, p. 1, 3, available from *www.whitehouse.gov/sites/default/files/counterterrorism_strategy.pdf*; *Quadrennial Defense Review Report*, Washington, DC: Department of Defense, February 2010, pp. v, 6, 15, available from *www.defense.gov/qdr/QDR%20as%20of%2026JAN10%200700. pdf*; Quadrennial Defense Review Independent Panel, *The QDR in Perspective: Meeting America's National Security Needs in the 21st Century, Final Report of the Quadrennial Defense Review Independent Panel*, Corrected Advance Copy, Washington, DC: United States Institute of Peace, 2010, p. 26.

2. As classically noted, a clear definition of the enemy and nature of war one fights are essential first principles for sound policy and strategy. See, Carl von Clausewitz, *On War*, Michael Howard and Peter Paret, eds. and trans., Princeton, NJ: Princeton University Press, 1976/1989, pp. 88-89; Sun Tzu, *The Art of War*, Thomas Cleary, trans., Boston, MA: Shambala, 2005, p. 53. The

June 2011 *National Strategy on Counterterrorism* defines this war in the following terms: "The United States deliberately uses the word 'war' to describe our relentless campaign against [al-Qaeda]. However, this administration has made it clear that we are not at war with the tactic of terrorism or the religion of Islam. We are at war with a specific organization—[al-Qaeda]," (p. 2). The scope of this [al-Qaeda] threat is more expansive than its core command and control, or al-Qaeda central, to include its affiliates and adherents. As further stated: "The preeminent security threat to the United States continues to be from **[al-Qaeda] and its affiliates and adherents,**" *National Strategy on Counterterrorism*, p. 3 (bold in original). This more expansive scope now includes what might be termed al-Qaedist groups and individuals—associated, affiliated, and inspired—who use violence to target the United States, its interests, allies, and other targets of opportunity (*Ibid.*, p. 3). Key definitions (*Ibid.*, p. 3) further clarify the scope of this adversary and nature of this war. [1] "*Associated Forces*" is "a legal term of art that refers to cobelligerents of al Qa'ida and the Taliban against whom the President is authorized to use force (including the authority to detain) based on the Authorization to Use Military Force, Pub.L.107-40, 115 Stat. 224 (2001)." [2] "Affiliates" includes "Associated Forces" but also includes "groups and individuals against whom the United States is not authorized to use force based on the authorities granted by the Authorization for the Use of Military Force, Pub.L.107-40, 115 Stat. 224 (2001). "The use of *Affiliates* in this strategy," the document continues, "is intended to reflect a broader category of entities against whom the United States must bring various elements of national power, as appropriate and consistent with the law, to counter the threat they pose." Finally, [3] "Adherents" are defined as "Individuals who have formed collaborative relationships with, act on behalf of, or are otherwise inspired to take action in furtherance of the goals of al-Qaeda—the organization and the ideology—including engaging in violence regardless of whether such violence is targeted at the United States, its citizens, or interests." A final official, illuminating definition of the enemy is provided by former 9/11 Commission co-chairs Thomas H. Kean and Lee Hamilton, "The [9/11] commission embraced a definition of the enemy as two pronged: 'al-Qaeda, a stateless network of terrorists that struck us on 9/11; and a radical ideological movement in the Islamic world, inspired in part by [al-Qaeda], which has spawned terrorist groups and violence across the globe.' We made a conscious decision to refer to the enemy as 'Islamist terrorism'—not as 'terrorism' the tactic, or 'Islam the religion'." (See Thomas H. Kean and Lee H. Hamilton *Without Precedent: The Inside Story of the 9/11 Commission*, New York: Alfred A. Knopf, 2006, p. 283.) For the likelihood that latent conflicts are beginning to emerge between the Departments of State and Defense as a result of this more expansive conception of terrorist opponent and the jurisdictional, diplomatic, strategic, and operational issues involved, see Charlie Savage, "Obama Adviser Discusses Using Military on Terrorists," *The New York Times*, September 16, 2011, available from *www.nytimes.com/2011/09/17/us/john-o-brennan-on-use-of-military-force-against-al-qaeda.html*.

3. National Commission on Terrorist Attacks Upon the United States, *Final Report of the National Commission on Terrorist Attacks Upon the United States*, New York: W. W. Norton, 2004, chap. 12 (hereafter *The 9/11 Commission Report*).

4. See, for example, Peter Bergen and Katherine Tiedemann, "Washington's Phantom War: The Effects of the Drone Program in Pakistan," *Foreign Affairs*, Vol. 90, No. 4, July/August 2011, pp. 12-18; "Al Qaeda Shadow of Former Self 10 Years After 9/11," Reuters, September 9, 2011, available from *http://www.reuters.com/article/2011/09/09/us-sept11-alqaeda-future-id USTRE7881DS20110909*; Greg Miller, "U.S. officials believe al-Qaeda on brink of collapse," *The Washington Post*, July 26, 2011, available from *www.washingtonpost.com/world/national-security/al-qaeda-could-collapse-us-officials-say/2011/07/21/gIQAFu2pbI_story.html*; "Charting the data for U.S. airstrikes in Pakistan, 2004-2011," *The Long War Journal*, available from *www.longwarjournal.org/pakistan-strikes.php*. Remarkably, just 5 months since the takedown of bin Laden, American-born Yemeni Anwar al-Awlaki—notorious for his effectiveness at radicalization and recruiting English-language Muslims living in Western societies—has met a similar fate. See CNN Wire Staff, "U.S. officials warn of possible retaliation after al Qaeda cleric is killed," September 30, 2011, available from *www.cnn.com/2011/09/30/world/africa/yemen-radical-cleric/*.

5. For a measured assessment that identifies notable achievements yet highlights continuing areas of vulnerability, see Bipartisan Policy Center, *Tenth Anniversary Report Card: The Status of the 9/11 Commission Recommendations*, Washington, DC: National Se-

curity Preparedness Group, September 2011, available from *www. bipartisanpolicy.org/library/report/tenth-anniversary-report-card-status-911-commission-recommendations;* Cheryl Pellerin, "Officials: Defense-Intelligence Integration Strongest Since 9/11," Armed Forces Press Service, September 8, 2011, available from *www.defense.gov/news/newsarticle.aspx?id=65279.*

6. The 10th-anniversary of the 9/11 terrorist attacks on the United States should have seen a catastrophic follow-on attack, but did not. Rather we witnessed a rather gaunt, ghostly, hunted, hidden shell of a savaged underground conspiratorial vanguard group whose singular accomplishment that day was to post a video entitled "The Dawn of Imminent Victory," to jihadist websites. New al-Qaeda emir Dr. Ayman al-Zawahiri appears in a still image, accompanied by audio. Footage is also presented of former terror master bin Laden, identical to that gathered by special operators in the May take-down in Abbotabad, Pakistan, but no longer muted, in which he warns Americans, among other things, of "falling slaves to corporations"as bin Laden himself in actuality falls slave to deep sea ocean currents and inevitable corporeal decomposition. And, of course, solidarity is expressed for the Arab revolutions; a nod toward defeating the United States in Iraq and Afghanistan; and . . . drum roll please. . . "the 9/11 attacks." One can only begin to imagine the signal intelligence (SIGINT) and human intelligence (HUMINT) operators slowly but surely tightening the noose and thus forcing continuing reliance on a practically-medieval courier network used to secretly send out that earth-shattering, momentous signifier of al-Qaeda's present incapacity (available from *www.bbc.co.uk/news/world-us-canada-14895727*).

7. Audrey K. Cronin, *How Terrorism Ends: Understanding the Decline and Demise of Terrorist Campaigns*, Princeton, NJ, and Oxford, MA: Princeton University Press, 2009/2011, p. 8. See also Antulio J. Echevarria, II, *Wars of Ideas and The War of Ideas*, Carlisle, PA: Strategic Studies Institute, U.S. Army War College, June 2008, pp. viii, 39, available from *www.StrategicStudiesInstitute.army.mil*, for explicit recognition of the importance of physical events that serve to undermine terrorist recruitment, organizational success, and the legitimizing of intellectual, ideological, or dogmatic-theological concepts and narratives.

8. Cronin, based on data trends ending c. 2008, severely underestimates the strategic potential of relentless hunting and decapitation of high value terrorist targets, and significantly overestimates the costs that she believes it may entail, which include the likely elevating of Osama bin Laden to the status of a martyred Muslim icon and the relative ease of generating new high value terrorist cadre. (see, e.g., pp. 177-179, 190, 194-195); This may be due to her underestimation of al-Qaeda's vanguardist ambitions and organizational structure that, while not tied to a single individual, presumes a battle-hardened, time-tested, absolutely loyal secret cadre capable of monopolizing and carrying out a global projection of strategic vision.

9. *Ibid.*, pp. 179-182. Defeating an adversary demands that one fully understand, master, and defeat an adversary's strategy (Sun Tzu, p. 35; Robert Kennedy, "The Elements of Strategic Thinking," in Gabriel Marcella, ed., *Teaching Strategy: Challenge and Response*, Carlisle, PA: Strategic Studies Institute, U.S. Army War College, March 2010, p. 16; Jarret Brachman, *Global Jihadism: theory and practice*, New York: Routledge, 2009, pp. 183-184). It is on these grounds that a deliberate, intentional, thoughtful U.S. policy of disaggregation has been suggested by scholars and many Western counterterrorism analysts as the *sine qua non* for countering al-Qaeda's principal strategy of aggregation. See, for example: Cronin, pp. 182, 193, 195; David C. Gompert and John Gordon, IV *et al., War by Other Means: Building Complete and Balanced Capabilities for Counterinsurgency*, Santa Monica, CA: RAND National Defense Research Institute, 2008, pp. 49-73; David Kilcullen, *The Accidental Guerrilla: Fighting Small Wars in the Midst of a Big One*, Oxford, UK: Oxford University Press, 2009 (esp. pp. 14-15, 292-293). For an excellent analysis of al-Qaeda's "double-bind" preventing it from aggregating with either local-national territorial insurgent movements or classical defensive jihad movements, see Vahid Brown, "Al-Qaeda Central and Local Affiliates," in Assaf Moghadam and Brian Fishman, eds., *Self-Inflicted Wounds: Debates and Divisions within al-Qaeda and its Periphery*, Harmony Project, West Point, NY: U.S. Military Academy, Combating Terrorism Center, December 16, 2010, pp. 69-99, available from *www.ctc. usma.edu*.

10. Cronin, pp. 191.

11. *Ibid.*, pp. 190-191. Like decapitation, Cronin significantly downplays the cumulative effects of repression for the viability of al-Qaeda's external operations capability. Again, in fairness to her, at the time of publication (c. 2009) the relentless, systematic, drone-based, high-value targeting campaign had barely just begun.

12. Cronin, p. 94; As David Blair states "Terrrorist movements across the world have a history of alienating their popular support by waging campaigns of indiscriminate murder." See "Al-Qaeda Founder Launches Fierce Attack on Osama bin Laden," *The Telegraph*, February 20, 2009, available from *www. telegraph.co.uk/news/worldnews/africaandindianocean/egypt/4736358/ Al-Qaeda-founder-launches-fierce-attack-on-Osama-bin-Laden.html*. For dramatic data on al-Qaeda's decline in support from three key bases: the Arab and Muslim populace, influential salafi Islamic scholars and clerics, and bona fide jihad-realist militants, see Rajeh Said, "Ten years after September 11th Attacks, al-Qaeda Lacks Popular Support," *Al-Shorfa.com*, September 9, 2011, available from *al-shorfa.com/cocoon/meii/xhtml/en_GB/features/meii/features/ main/2011/09/09/feature*.

13. See Alia Brahimi, "Crushed in the Shadows: Why Al Qaeda will Lose the War of Ideas," *Studies in Conflict and Terrorism*," Vol. 33, 2010, pp. 93-110, for how the devolution of operational control to local affiliates and adherents in Iraq dramatically undercut al-Qaeda's broader strategic objectives.

14. Cronin, Chap. 4, pp. 183-186.

15. See for example, Joas Wagemakers, "Invoking Zarqawi: Abu al-Maqdisi's Jihad Decifit," *CTC Sentinel*, Vol. 2, No. 6, June 2009, pp. 14-17, for a strategically consequential example of how divisions arose pitting the highly-credentialed salafi scholar al-Maqdisi, with his rigid commitment to binding shari'a-based rules for waging jihad, against those claiming to prove their "real" jihadi credentials through their willingness to practice and justify brutally savage sectarian violence. For how this operational devolution is manifest in meta-narratives that elevate opportunistic constructions of sacred sources that simultaneously demote scholarly acumen in favor of violent praxis, see Akil N. Awa, "Success of the Meta-Narrative: How Jihadists Maintain Legitimacy," *CTC*

Sentinel, Vol. 2, No. 11, November 2009, pp. 6-8, available from *www.ctc.usma.edu*.

16. *Ibid.*, p. 95; See especially, Brian Fishman and Assaf Mogh-adam, "Do Jihadi and Islamist Divisions Matter? Implications for Policy and Strategy," in Moghadam and Fishman, eds., *Self-In-flicted Wounds*, pp. 224-240, for a deeply insightful description of potential implosion tactics applicable to al-Qaeda.

17. Cronin, p. 95.

18. Cronin's approach is usefully complemented by an ex-tremely compelling account of traditional deterrence theory ex-tended to counterterrorism advocated by Alex S. Wilner, "Deter-ring the Undeterrable: Coercion, Denial and Delegitimation in Counterterrorism," *Journal of Strategic Studies*, Vol. 34, No. 1, 2011, pp. 3-37, available from *dx.doi.org/10.1080/01402390.2011.541760*.

19. The structure of this narrative is Islam's very self-under-standing as the exclusive agent on earth of Allah's will manifest as Islam's glorious rise, divinely-inspired spread, present-day in-glorious absence, and a proposed path for its restoration to divine glory. In apologetic writings, one first encounters a benedictory introduction thanking Allah, supreme God of the worlds, for all that is, and all that is Good. Immediately following, one is ap-prised of a Past-Perfect Islamic glorious golden age. Third, an ac-count of "The Fall" is provided that is largely a dystopian odyssey involving Western cultural modernity being imposed as a preda-tory colonial plot to rip apart, weaken, and disable the Umma. Fourth, the question "What is to be done?" is posed and a singular answer offered: Islam. Specifically, one must reinstitute the rule of Allah's shari'a through the twin means of *da'wa* (preaching, the call) and jihad. This demand to resurrect the religious prescription to wage military jihad is a key dividing line that separates jihadi and non-jihadi Islam and, in the opinion of the present author, the religious prescription is indeed religiously-grounded and thus, the fifth and sixth components are essential to the comple-tion of the specifically jihadi narrative. Fifth, how it is to be done *lawfully*; and sixth, *how it is not to be done unlawfully*. For an excel-lent example of this six-part narrative structure in the writing of one of the most important of the revisionist jihad-realist scholars, see Sayyid al-Imam Abd-al-Aziz al-Sharif, *Doctrine of Rationaliza-*

tion (i.e., Right Guidance) for Jihad Activity in Egypt and the World (Wathiqat Tarshid Al-'Aml Al-Jihadi fi Misr w'Al-Alam), November 2007, serialized in *Al-Sharq al-Awsat in Arabic* and partially available on *www.opensource.gov*, Part 1. Crucial here is that (1) jihad is regarded as including an armed, military dimension; and, (2) its legal parameters precisely specified. The purpose of the present monograph is to demonstrate that it is possible to disable al-Qaeda's reign of terror *on these grounds*, i.e., the jurisprudence of lawful military jihad. This does not require a counternarrative, which would in effect amount to an attempted demythologization of a religious faith whose overwhelming majority of adherents — despite maintaining faith in the first three elements of the above narrative — regard terrorism directed at innocent civilian noncombatants — Muslim and non-Muslim — as morally abhorrent, repulsive, murderous, and un-Islamic.

20. For the Quranic injunction to fight in the way of Allah to make Allah's word supreme, including nonmartial forms of such struggling and striving, see for example Abdullah Yusuf Ali, *The Meaning of the Holy Qur'an*, New Ed. with Rev. Trans. and Commentary, Brentwood, MD: Amana Corporation, 1992, 2:148, 190-193, 216-218, 246, 256, 262-263; 3:13, 104, 121-123, 134-136, 150-58, 167-171, 195; 4:71-78, 89-96; 5:35; 8:12-19,30, 38-48, 59-75; 9:1-16, 20-24, 36-49, 111, 123; 22:39-41, 58-59, 78; 29:68-69; 33:18-27, 60-62; 47:4-11, 20, 33-38; 48:15-29; 49:15; 57:10; 59:2-14; 60:1, 7-9; 61:4, 11-13; 73:20. This authoritative support for the superlative nature and religious prescription to wage the military jihad is also explicit in many passages in the two most authoritatively-binding hadith collections — Sahih Al-Bukhari, and Sahih Muslim. See for example, *Sahih Al-Bukhari (The Translation of the Meanings of Sahih Al-Bukhari)*, Dr. Muhammad Muhsin Khan, trans., Riyadh: Saudi Arabia: Darussalam, 1997, Vol. 4, Book 56, "The Book of Jihad" (2782-3090): 2783-2785, 2787-2789, 2791, 2792-2805, 2808-2810, 2811, 2813-2820, 2824-2829, 2831-2835, 2837-2839, 2841, 2843-2847, 2849-2853, 2860-2861, 2863-2864, 2874-2884, 2887-2891, 2892-2895, 2897-2899, 2902-2904, 2906, 2909-2910, 2913, 2919-2922, 2924-2935, 2942-2950, 2954, 2961-2967, 2970-2973, 2975, 2977-2978, 2981, 2986, 2990-2991, 2995, 2997, 3002-3004, 3006-3010, 3012, 3016-3018, 3020-3025-3034, 3037, 3039, 3041-3043, 3045-3048, 3051-3052, 3057, 3061-3069, 3073, 3074-3077, 3081-3084,3087-3088. For what might be termed 'ultra-jihad', see 2887, 2927-2930, 2943, 2945-46, 2961-62, 2966, 2972, 3022, 3043, 3051, 3076, 3077; 2966, 3025 ("Paradise

under the Shade of Swords"); 2792-2798 ("Martyrdom, and Paradise"); 2833-2834 ("Actual Fighters, and Rewards"). See also Sahih Al-Bukhari, Vol. 1, Book 2, "The Book of Belief" (aman), chapter 26, #36, p. 73. In *Sahih Muslim*, Abdul Hamid Siddiqi, trans., Sh. Muhammad Ashraf: Lahore, Pakistan, 2004, Vol. 3, Book 10, *"Kitab al-Jihad"* (4292-4472): 4292, 4294, 4297-4300, 4311, 4313-4315, 4319, 4321-4325, 4327-4330, 4332-4341, 4344-4349, 4353-4355, 4357-4358, 4360-4361, 4363-4366, 4368, 4370, 4372-4375, 4377, 4385, 4388-4390, 4392-4396, 4405-4406, 4413, 4429, 4437-4441, 4445-4447, 4452-4453, 4456-4457, 4462, 4464-4470, 4472; and, for the most militant of the martial jihad traditions, see 4292, 4294, 4340-4341, 4344, 4347, 4363, 4366, 4370, 4372, 4375, 4385, 4388-4393, 4395-96, 4405, 4406, 4413, 4437-4447 , esp. 4462-4470, 4472. The religious prescription to wage military jihad is also found outside the "Book of Jihad" in the "Book of Faith" (*aman*), *Sahih Muslim*, Vol. 1, Chap. 9, "Command for Fighting Against the People So Long as They Do Not Profess That There is No God But Allah and Muhammad is His Messenger," # 30-34 (pp. 16-17). The crux of the martyrological covenant is crisply captured in this classical Qur'anic *ayah*, a kind of "jihadi covenant" (Ali, pp. 470-471, 9:111): "Allah hath purchased of the Believers their persons and their goods; For theirs (in return) is the Garden (of Paradise): They fight in His Cause, and slay and are slain: A promise binding on Him In Truth, through the Law, The Gospel, and the Qur'an. And who is more faithful to His Covenant than Allah? Then rejoice in the bargain which ye have concluded: That is the achievement supreme."

Despite the fact Islam is by wide consensus viewed to rest on five pillars—creed, prayer, alms, fasting on Ramadan, and participation in the Hajj—the classical sources are not in agreement. For example, *Sahih Muslim*, Vol. 1, "The Book of Faith," chap. 6, pp. 10-11, #21, states: "It is reported on the authority of Ta'us that a man said to Abdullah son of Umar (may Allah be pleased with him): Why don't you carry out a military expedition? Upon which he replied: I heard the Messenger of Allah (may peace be upon him) say: Verily, al-Islam is founded on five (pillars): testifying the fact that there is no god but Allah, establishment of prayer, payment of Zakat, fast of Ramadan and Pilgrimage to the House." In *Sahih Al-Bukhari*, Vol. 1, Book 2, "The Book of Faith," chapter 18, #26, it reports the following tradition: "Narrated Abu Jurairah: Allah's Messenger [peace be upon him] was asked, "What is the best deed?" He replied, "To believe in Allah and His Messenger (Muhammad)[peace be upon him]." The questioner then asked,

"What is the next [in goodness]?" He replied, "To participate in *Jihad* [holy fighting] in Allah's Cause."

21. For select contributions to this vast and ever-growing literature touting the utility of various non-jihadi counternarrative strategies, techniques, and recipes—often imagined as silver bullets—for disabusing the Muslim world of such "myths," "narratives," "ideologies," "religious ideologies," and other foibles allegedly at the heart of their distorted and contorted "occidentalist" imagination of the West, see Kenneth Payne, "Winning the Battle of Ideas: Propaganda, Ideology, and Terror," *Studies in Conflict and Terrorism*, Vol. 32, 2009, pp. 109-138; William D. Casebeer and James A Russell, "Storytelling and Terrorism: Towards a Comprehensive 'Counter-Narrative' Strategy," *Strategic Insights*, Vol. 4, No. 3, March 2005, available from *www.au.af.mil/au/awc/awcgate/nps/casebeer_mar05.pdf*; Angela Trethewey, Steven R. Corman, "Out of Their Heads and into Their Conversation: Countering Extremist Ideology," Consortium for Strategic Communication, Phoenix, AZ: Arizona State University, Report #0902, September 14, 2009, available from *comops.org/article/123.pdf*; Bud Goodall, Angela Trethewey, and Kelly McDonald, "Strategic Ambiguity, Communication, and Public Diplomacy in an Uncertain World: Principles and Practices," Consortium for Strategic Communication, Phoenix, AZ: Arizona State University, Report #0604, June 21, 2006, available from *comops.org/article/116.pdf*; H. L. Goodall, Jr., "Why We Must Win the War on Terror: Communication, Narrative, and the Future of National Security," *Qualitative Inquiry*, Vol. 12, No. 1, February 2006, pp. 30-59; Tom Quiqqin, "Understanding al-Qaeda's Ideology for Counter-Narrative Work," *Perspectives on Terrorism*, Vol. 3, No. 2, August 2009, pp. 18-35, available from *www.terrorismanalysts.com*. Heather S. Gregg, "Fighting the Jihad of the Pen: Countering Revolutionary Islam's Ideology," *Terrorism and Political Violence*, Vol. 22, 2010, pp. 292-314; Simon Cottee, "Mind Slaughter: The Neutralizations of *Jihadi* Salafism," *Studies in Conflict and Terrorism*, Vol. 33, 2010, pp. 330-352; Allison G. Smith, "From Words to Action: Exploring the Relationship between a Group's Value Preferences and Its Liklihood of Engaging in Terrorism," *Studies in Conflict and Terrorism*, Vol. 27, 2004, pp. 409-437.

Though this work is admirable in many respects, Burki's implicit assumption (Shireen K. Burki, "Ceding the Ideological Battlefield to Al Qaeda: The Absence of an Effective U.S Information

Warfare Strategy," *Comparative Strategy*, Vol. 38, 2009, pp. 349-366) that Islamic supremacism begins with medieval *Hanbali Fiqh* luminary Ibn Taymiyyah, (see p. 350), and not al-Qaeda per se, but a shifting mosaic of fundamentalist signifiers must be delegitimated—i.e., "fundamentalist Islam" (p. 357). "Once the enemy has been correctly, and publicly, identified as Islamic fundamentalists (i.e., Wahhabists, Salafists, and others). . . a certain type of virulent Islamic ideology derivative of *Hanbali Fiqh*," (p. 360); "Salafist/ Wahhabi ideology," (p. 362) — unnecessarily broadens the enemy to include enormous chunks of fundamentalist adherents whose propensity for terrorism, despite intolerance and supremacism, is extremely questionable.

For scholarly analyses of Salafism and Wahhabism, see for example Roel Meijer, ed., *Global Salafism: Islam's New Religious Movement*, New York: Columbia University Press, 2009 generally, but especially Thomas Hegghammer, "Jihadi-Salafis or Revolutionaries? On Religion and Politics in the Study of Militant Islamism," Meijer, ed., *Global Salafism*, pp. 244-266; Quintan Wiktorowicz, "Anatomy of the Salafi Movement," *Studies in Conflict and Terrorism*," Vol. 29, 2006, pp. 207-239; International Crisis Group, "Indonesia Backgrounder: Why Salafism and Terrorism Mostly Don't Mix," September 13, 2004, available from *www.crisisgroup. org*; Natana J. Delong-Bas, *Wahhabi Islam: From Revival and Reform to Global Jihad*, New York: Oxford University Press, 2004; Christina Hellmich, "Creating the Ideology of Al Qaeda: From Hypocrites to Salafi Jihadis," *Studies in Conflict and Terrorism*, Vol. 31, 2008, esp. pp. 114-119, for a devastatingly-accurate critique of what the author terms "outside-in" scholarship on al-Qaeda, and key failures in conceptualizing Salafism, so-called Wahhabism, and in consulting primary sources such as Ibn Taymiyyah's actual *Fatawa* or al-Wahhab's actual theological demands, instead of exclusively consulting the group-think that mostly rests on often-ignorant or biased commentary. For what the present author regards as the most sophisticated, persuasive, and nuanced critique of the presumption of a fundamentalist-terrorist nexus — whether Salafi, Wahhabi, or otherwise — see Muhammad Haniff Bin-Hassan, "Key Considerations in Counterideological Work against Terrorist Ideology," *Studies in Conflict and Terrorism*, Vol. 29, 2006, esp. pp. 541-547.

22. Bin Hassan, "Key Considerations in Counterideological Work against Terrorist Ideology," pp. 537-538, advocates a "theological and juristic approach" virtually identical to that developed by the present author. However, the explicit recognition of jihad as a binding religious prescription (jihad realist) and Islamic jurisprudence (jurisprudential) or sacred law and shari'a methodology concerning behavioral proscriptions, prescriptions, and a continuum of lawful conduct—from obligatory (*fard*) to forbidden (*haram*) and stages in-between—is the vital center-of-gravity identified in the present author's approach. "Theological" too often connotes more abstract, scholarly investigations into the manner in which the godhead exists, relates to the world and to man in the world, as well as debates over the relative rights of human reason versus faith in discerning those properties.

What is key in the above approach is clearly understood by both bin Hassan, "Key Considerations in Counterideological Work against Terrorist Ideology," p. 531, and Wilner, "Deterring the Undeterrable," pp. 26-31, who both amply demonstrate the vital importance of attacking terrorist beliefs about their own legal and moral legitimacy. For bin Hassan, a successful terrorist act rests on three factors: opportunity (i.e., available targets), capability (i.e., money, training, weapons, recruits), and motivation (i.e., ideological and nonideological drivers), p. 531. Citing General William Slim, commander of the Fourteenth Army in Burma during World War II, bin Hassan identifies "morale"—a crucial factor for the willful disposition of the fighter—as presuming three key dimensions: *intellectual* confidence that "the goal can be attained," *material* confidence that "the means of attaining the goal are available," and *spiritual* confidence "that the cause is just," p. 534. Translated in the vernacular of shari'a-based criteria for judging the legality of a jihad, the first two requirements—available means and probable success—deal with the *pragmatics* of jihad (i.e., Can it be done? Do the benefits outweigh the costs for the Umma?). The third requirement, concerns the *legality* or Islamic *legitimacy* of jihad (i.e., Is it just? *Should* it be done? Does the shari'a justify this jihad?). Wilner, extending deterrence theory to counterterrorism also identifies three key bases underpinning the terrorist cost/benefit calculus, two rooted in pragmatics, and the third—legitimation (see esp. pp. 26-31)—that demands that terrorist actors root their actions in the moral and legal demands of Islamic shari'a.

23. Majid Khadduri, *War and Peace in the Law of Islam*, Baltimore, MD: Johns Hopkins Press, 1955, pp. 14-18.

24. See Sherifa Zuhur, *Precision in the Global War on Terror: Inciting Muslims Through the War of Ideas*, Carlisle, PA: Strategic Studies Institute, U.S. Army War College, April 2008, available from *www.StrategicStudiesInstitute.army.mil*, for an outstanding contribution designed to disabuse ignorant, opportunistic, or otherwise dangerously-off-the-mark scholars from egregious stereotypes and ignorant formulations of essential Islamic and Islamist beliefs, practices, concepts, and values. Armed with an accurate mapping of actual Islam and Islamism, one can both establish the trusted long-term networks essential to the *intra*-civilizational debates informing Western and Islamic sociocultural life, and partially mitigate the damage done to such a project by those seeking, on the basis of the wildest and most erroneous premises, an *inter*-civilizational war.

25. For academic accounts of this binding religious prescription, see for example: E. Tyan, "Djihad," *Encyclopedia of Islam*, New Ed., Leiden, UK: E. J. Brill, 1965; David Cook, *Understanding Jihad*, Berkeley, CA: University of California Press, 2005; W. Gardner, "Jihad," *The Moslem World*, Vol. 2, 1912, pp. 347-357; Majid Khadduri, *War and Peace in the Law of Islam*, Baltimore, MD: Johns Hopkins Press, 1955, Book II, The Law of War: The Jihad, pp. 51-137; Rudolph Peters, ed., *Jihad: In Classical and Modern Islam: A Reader*, 2nd Ed., Princeton, NJ: Marcus Wiener, 2005; Michael Bonner, *Jihad in Islamic History: Doctrines and Practice*, Princeton, NJ: Princeton University Press, 2006; Richard Bonney, *Jihad: From Qur'an to bin Laden*, New York: Palgrave Macmillan, 2004; Andrew Bostom, ed., *The Legacy of Jihad: Islamic Holy War and the Fate of Non-Muslims*, Amherst, NY: Prometheus, 2005; Stephen Collins Coughlin, *"To Our Great Detriment": Ignoring What Extremists Say About Jihad,* Unclassified Master's thesis submitted to the faculty of the National Defense Intelligence College, July 2007; Reuven Firestone, *Jihad: The Origin of Holy War in Islam*, New York: Oxford University Press, 1999; William Gawthorp, "Dogmatic Basis of Jihad and Martyrdom," *Small Wars Journal*, July 6, 2011, available from s*mallwarsjournal.com/jrnl/art/dogmatic-basis-of-jihad-and-martyrdom*, presents a virtual inventory of jihad and martyrdom-authorizing statements and legal requirements contained in the classical sources and commentary.

26. See also Alia Brahimi, "Crushed in the Shadows: Why Al Qaeda Will Lose the War of Ideas," *Studies in Conflict and Terrorism*, Vol. 33, 2010, p. 96, for insistence on placing al-Qaeda's terrorism within the legal framework of a legitimately declared and fought defensive jihad. The connection between the imperative to wage jihad, and the requirement that it be waged lawfully, is evident in the following quote from Sayyid Imam, whose works will be discussed at length (see Sayyid Imam, *Exposure of the Exoneration Book Al-Ta'riya li Kitab Al-Tabri'ya*, "Twelfth Episode of Sayyid Imam: Al-Zawahiri had no Prior Knowledge of 09/11," appearing in *Al Misri Al Yawm* in Arabic December 1, 2008 by Ahmad Al-Khatib, "The Second man in Al-Qai'ida Turned Osama Bin Ladin from a Traitor to a Mujahid to Inherit the Allegiance of his Followers," Part 12, p. 6: "Jihad for Allah's sake is just, but do not allow those people and their likes to auctioneer with this noble cause. They push youths to extreme sacrifices and they bring major catastrophes on the Muslims even though they most [sic] careful about their personal safety and about reaping benefits without realizing the least benefit for Islam and the Muslims."

27. Peter Bergen and Paul Cruickshank, "The Unraveling: Al Qaeda's revolt against bin Laden," *The New Republic*, June 11, 2008, p. 17.

28. *Ibid.*, p. 20.

29. *Ibid.*

30. *Ibid.*, p. 18.

31. While insufficient in itself, the importance of the legal repudiation of al-Qaeda arising from jihad-realist militants committed to rigorous adherence to shari'a requirements, is a necessary condition for undercutting any conceivable religious warrant. As these authors state: "[T]he repudiation of Al Qaeda's leaders by its former religious, military, and political guides will help hasten the implosion of the jihadist terrorist movement. . . . And, given the religio-ideological basis of Al Qaeda's jihad, the religious condemnation now being offered by scholars and fighters once close to the organization is arguably the most important development in stopping the group's spread since September 11," *Ibid.*,

p. 21. Quoting Kamal El Helbay, a Muslim Brotherhood leader who helped wrest the Finsbury Park, London mosque from its shari'a violating former firebrand al-Qaedists': "No government, no police force, is achieving what these [religious] scholars are achieving. To defeat terrorism, to convince the radicals . . . you have to persuade them that theirs is not the path to paradise," *Ibid.*, p. 21. The difficulty of this task of differentiating lawful jihad from unlawful murderous terrorism remains, however, for it is not just a matter of convincing, but of first penetrating an extremist, arrogant, hostile, self-righteous mindset, often entirely ignorant of crucial Islamic tenets, and one that is self-insulating since all scholars, clerics, and observant Muslims not engaged in the terrorist project are viewed as internal enemies. For a real sense of the difficulty facing these salafi sheiks, even highly-regarded ones, on the front lines — not only among the youth, but from among fellow sheikhs, see the article by Sheikh Salman al-Oadah, and Comments by Shaykh Yaser Birjas in "UPDATE: Standing United Against Terrorism & Al-Qaeda – Salman al-Oudah (with Yasir Qadhi, Yaser Birjas, Tawfique Chowdhurry, and Waleed Basyouni), *http://muslimmatters.org/2009/10/12/standing-united-against-terrorism-al-qaeda-salman-al-awdah-with-yasir-qadhi-and-yaser-birjas/*.

32. Islamic jurisprudence, which presumes a foundation in *Fiqh* — the science of shari'a (sacred Law) — is, as in other religious and secular traditions, highly specialized and contentious owing to differing traditions and principles of legal interpretation. The authority of a given legal scholar resides in his proven expertise in the sources and methods of the shari'a. The four traditional sources for shari'a comprise, in order of their authority: *Qur'an* (Islamic sacred scripture), *Ahadith* (traditions of varying soundness and quality concerning what Prophet Muhammad, and also his earliest companions, said and did), *Ijma* (unanimous scholarly consensus, which functions like precedent), and *Qiyas* (the use of simile or analogical reasoning). In addition, *Tafsir* (Qur'anic commentaries), *Handbooks* (handbooks of the various legal schools, e.g., Hannafi, Maliki, Shafi'i, Hanbali, that present binding law), and *Fatawa* (compendia containing authoritative legal opinions or verdicts) are used. The range of legal/moral permissibility of a given action is five-fold: [1] absolutely required or commanded (*fard*); [2] recommended, but not required (*mustahabb*); [3] indifferent, neutral, permissible (*mubah*); [4] discouraged or reprehensible,

but not forbidden (*makruh*); [5] absolutely and explicitly forbidden because both sinful and criminal (*haram*). See especially John Kelsay, *Arguing the Just War in Islam*, Cambridge, MA: Harvard University Press, 2007, chap. 2, "Shari'a Reasoning," pp. 43-96; "Shari'a" entry in *Encylopedia of Islam*, New Ed., C. Bosworth, E. Donzel, W. Heirichs, and G. Leconte, eds., Vol. 9, Leiden, UK: E. J. Brill, 1996, pp. 321-328. Because of the enormous stature of the arch-traditionalist, originalist *Hanbali Fiqh* that is upheld in Saudi Arabia, the more conservative Gulf countries, and among jihad-realist scholars and militants, the most damning case against al-Qaeda arises when this jurisprudential tradition, which uses the two "primary" and most authoritative sources (*Qur'an, Ahadith*) determines that absolutely forbidden sinful, criminal (*haram*) violations of the shari'a have occurred. The three key luminaries of the *Hanbali* school: its namesake Ibn Hanbal (d. 855); the great medieval scholar and 'jihadist' Ahmad Ibn Taymiyya (d. 1328); and Muhammad bin Abd al-Wahhab, namesake for the so-called Hanbalite 'Wahhabi' school (d. 1792); form a theologico-juridico backbone against whom contemporary al-Qaedist terrorists run afoul, because the teachings of these three key luminaries readily condemn al Qaeda of abominable acts in the strictest Islamic terms. For a survey of Hanbali scholars, see, H. Laoust, "Hanabila" in *The Encyclopedia of Islam*, New Ed., B. Lewis, V. L. Menage, Ch. Pellat, and J. Schacht, eds., Leiden, UK: E. J. Brill, 1971, Vol. 3, pp. 158-162.

33. Owing to the recognized stature of these jihad-realist authorities, and available English-language translations, the following works by present and former members of armed 'jihadist' organizations were consulted. For the Libyan Islamic Fighting Group (LIFG): Libyan Islamic Fighting Group (LIFG), *A Selected Translation of the LIFG Recantation Document*, Transl. Mohammed Ali Musawi, Quilliam Foundation, available from *http://www. quilliamfoundation.org/images/a_selected_translation_of_the_lifg.pdf,* 2009. Each work provides a translation of the introductory passages, which are key to understanding the document's intentions and context, as well as providing a translation of the summary of each chapter that appears in the original Arabic. The document, *Revisionist [or Corrective] Studies of the Concepts of Jihad, Hisbah [Accountability], and Takfir [Judging others' 'Muslimness']* — is approximately 400 pages organized in nine chapters and made available to the public on September 6, 2009. Its six authors comprise the LIFG's highest echelon leadership: current emir, Abdul

Hakim al-Khwailidi Balhaj, aka: Abu Abdullah al-Sadiq; deputy emir, Khalid Muhammad Al-Sharif; spiritual leader, Sami Mustafa Al-Saadi, aka: Abu al-Munzir al Saaidi; its first emir, Miftah al-Mbruk al-Thawadi, aka: Abdul Ghaffar; military commander, Musafah Al-Said Qunayid, aka: Abu al-Zubair; and, Abdul Wahhab Muhammad Qayid, aka: Abu Idris (remarkably, also the elder brother of senior al-Qaeda ideologue Abu Yahya al-Libi). The original Arabic text is available online from *www.akhbar-libyaonline.com*. For background, commentary, and additional analysis, see "The Daily Star: Deradicalizing Jihadists, the Libyan Way," April 26, 2010, available from *www.opensource.gov*; Noman Benotman, "Al-Qaeda: Your Armed Struggle is Over," September 10, 2010, available from *www.quilliamfoundation.org/ images/stories/pdfs/letter-to-bin-laden.pdf*; Rania Karam, "Former LIFG leader: Bin Laden lacks Islamic authority to wage 'Western Jihad," May 5, 2010, available from *www.magharaebia.com*; Kamil al Tawil (Camille Tawil), "Noman Benotman criticizes al-Qaeda in bin Laden letter," September 23, 2010, available from *www.magharebia.com*; Rania Karam, "Former LIFG leader questions bin Laden rationale," April 29, 2010, available from *al-shorfa.com*; *Kamil al Tawil* (Camille Tawil), "Al-Qaeda yet to respond to corrective studies forbidding killing of civilians," September 15, 2009, available from *al-shorfa.com*; Camille Tawil, "Libya closes the case of the Libyan Islamic Fighting Group," March 30, 2010, available from *al-shorfa.com*; Nic Robertson and Paul Cruickshank, "In bid to thwart al Qaeda, Libya frees three leaders of jihadist group," March 23, 2010, available from *edition.cnn.com/2010/WORLD/africa/03/23/libya.jihadist.group*; Vahid Brown, "A First Look at the LIFG Revisions," September 14, 2009, available from *www.jihadica.com/a-first-look-at-the-lifg-revisions/*; Camille Tawil, "The Libyan Islamic Fighting Group's revisions: one year later," July 23, 2010, available from *www.magharebia.com*; Jarret Brachman, "Why the LIFG's Revisions are Falling on Our Deaf Ears," September 21, 2009, available from *jarretbrachman.net/?p=1036*; Thomas Hegghammer, "Libyan Jihad Revisions," September 8, 2009, available from *www.jihadica. com/libyan-jihad-revisions/*; Camille Tawil, "Libyan Islamists Back Away from al-Qaeda Merger in Reconciliation with Qaddafi Regime," *Terrorism Monitor*, Vol.7, No. 17, June 18, 2009, available from *www.jamestown.org*; Jarret Brachman, "Abu Yahya al-Libi's 'Human Shields in Modern Jihad'," *CTC Sentinel*, Vol. 1, No. 6, May 2008, pp. 1-4, available from *www.ctc.usma.edu*; Alison Par-

40

geter, "LIFG Revisions Unlikely to Reduce Jihadist Violence," *CTC Sentinel*, Vol. 2, No. 10, October 2009, pp. 7-9, available from *www.ctc.usma.edu*; Paul Cruickshank, "LIFG Revisions Posing Critical Challenge to al-Qaeda," *CTC Sentinel*, Vol. 2, No. 12, December 2009, pp. 5-8, available from *www.ctc.usma.edu*; Ian Black, "Libya's jihadis reject violence as leader bids for acceptance," September 4, 2009, available from *www.guardian.co.uk/world/2009/sep/04/libyan-islamist-fighters-reject-violence*; *Oea Online*, "Libyan Islamists' ideology revision serialization to start 6 Sep-paper," (Text of report by Libyan pro-government newspaper *Oea: "Oea* will, as of tomorrow [Sunday 6 September 2009], begin a serialization of the ideological revisions 'corrective studies' prepared recently by the Libyan Islamic Fighting Group [LIFG]"),September 6, 2009, available from *www.opensource.gov*; Camille Tawil, "Libyan Islamist Criticizes Tripoli's Refusal to Release the Libyan Islamic Fighting Group Prisoners," *Al Hayah* Online in Arabic, "Report by Kamil al-Tawil, 'Libyan Islamist Criticizes Tripoli's Refusal to Release the Libyan Islamic Fighting Group's Prisoners'," February 22, 2010, available from *www.opensource.gov*; *BBC Monitoring* in Arabic, "BBC Monitoring: Review of al-Qaeda Activities in North Africa 16 February-1 March [20]11," available from *www.opensource.gov*; Paul Cruickshank, "How Muslim Extremists are turning on Osama Bin Laden," June 7, 2008, available from *www.nydailynews.com*.

For the Egyptian Islamic Jihad organization, the following sources by, or commentary on Sayyid al-Imam Abd-al-Aziz al-Sharif's (aka Dr. Fadl, or, Shaykh Abd-al-Qadir Bin-Abd-al-Aziz) key jihad-realist revisionist works are: Omar Ashour, The De-Radicalization of Jihadists: Transforming Armed Islamist Movements, *The De-Radicalization of Jihadists: Transforming Armed Islamist Movements,* New York: Routledge, 2009, esp. Chaps. 3, 5. For brief biographical details on Sayyid Imam, see *Al-Sharq al-Awsat Online* in Arabic, "Report Lists Stages in Life, Career of Egypt's Jihad Group Leader Dr. Fadl" and *Al-Sharq al-Awsat* Online in Arabic, "Report: Seven Places Which Made Up Dr. Fadl's Life, the First Amir of Egyptian 'Jihad' Organization," November 19, 2009, available from *www.opensource.gov*. For publicity for the revisions, see *Al-Misri al-Yawm*, "Detained Egyptian Islamist leader urges 'rationalization' of jihad activity," *Al-Misri al-Yawm* in Arabic, text of report by Ahmad al-Khatib: "Faqih of [Egyptian] Jihad Organization to announce within days a document on 'rationalizing jihadist actions'," May 6, 2007, available from *www.opensource*.

gov; *Al-Sharq al-Wasat*, "Egyptian Islamic Group 'Theoretician' Supports Call for 'Rationalized' Jihad," *Al-Sharq al-Wasat* in Arabic article by Abdu Zaynah: "'Al-Jama'ah al-Islamiyah' Theoretician in Egypt Supports al-Qaeda Call for Ending Violence," May 13, 2007, available from *www.opensource.gov*; *Al-Misri al-Yawm*, "Egyptian Islamist lawyer says al-Qaedah to carry out religious revisions–paper," and *Al Misri al-Yawm* in Arabic excerpt from report by Ahmad al-Khatib: "Jihad Organization leaders unanimously approve *Fiqh* [Islamic jurisprudence] revisions," November 3, 2007, available from *www.opensource.gov*.

For the two key texts containing the legal requisites of lawful jihad: [1] Sayyid Imam, *Doctrine of Rationalization [i.e., Right Guidance] for Jihad Activity in Egypt and the World (Wathiqat Tarshid Al-'Aml Al-Jihadi fi Misr w'Al-Alam)*, November 2007, serialized in *Al-Sharq al-Awsat in Arabic* and partially available on *www.opensource.gov*; [2] Sayyid Imam, *Exposure of the Exoneration Book* [Al-Ta'riya li Kitab Al-Tabri'ya], completed by the author March 25, 2008, and published in 13-parts in Arabic by *Al-Misri Al-Yawm*, between November 18-December 2, 2008, available from *www.opensource.gov*. See Daniel Lav, "An In-Depth Summary of Sayyid Imam's New Polemic Against Al-Qaeda, 'Exposing the Exoneration,' February 23, 2009, available from *www.memri.org*, for an accurate summary of several key points made in the latter text.

Though 'Rationalization' does indeed contain occasional needless ad hominem attacks, three points are worth mentioning. First, a careful reading of both texts places these remarks in proper context and though perhaps unwise and distracting, they do not invalidate Sayyid Imam's key legal criticisms. Second, the vast majority of these ad hominem assaults are directed at Ayman al-Zawahiri's trustworthiness. To the extent that honesty, trustworthiness, and commitment to truthfulness are essential dispositional qualities for a person claiming ultimate concern for shari'a, evidence to the contrary is potentially devastating. It suggests that legal errors do not arise merely from inaccurate, ignorant, or invalid inference, but from intentional, willful deception. The original "Exposure" book consists of four interlinked chapters, one of which focuses virtually exclusively on what Sayyid Imam deems "theological inaccuracies," while the other three deal with questions bearing directly on motive and character. The linkage of the first two chapters is represented thusly, "You also ascertain the veracity of what I stated at the start of this chapter [two] in citing predecessor ulemas as saying that 'the statements of a liar and debauchee are not accepted in religion'. I have demonstrated in the first chapter that Al-Zawahiri is a liar who invents and fabricates. So what did that liar do when he issued fatwas about Allah's religion? You have seen in this chapter [two] how he perpetrated monstrosities and heresies that contradict the Shari'a of Islam. His monstrosities followed one another until they formed a criminal doctrine that allows wholesale killings under various pretexts and justifications. . . . Al-Zawahiri ought to have called his book 'The Justification' rather than 'The Exoneration'. The justification they sought to make for their criminal behavior rightly sets the foundation for the school of 'Ignorance and Crime in Jihad' in our times" (Sayyid Imam, "Exposure," Part 7, p. 2). And third, Sayyid Imam constructs a coherent explanation that explains both legal inaccuracies and intentional deception: that 9/11 and al-Qaeda represent in their essential core the personal vendetta of Osama bin Laden, and those whose agendas converged with his, e.g., Khalid Shaik Muhammad, to inflict the greatest loss of life possible on the United States. Ayman al-Zawahiri's legal function then, in Sayyid Imam's opinion, is to produce 'jurisprudence of justification' legalizing what amounts to a "corrupt doctrine about excessiveness in wholesale killing" or "a corrupt deviate doctrine to entrench excessiveness in spilling of blood, . . . This corrupt doctrine is what some call 'al-Qaeda ideology'" (Sayyid Imam, "Exposure," Part 2, pp. 1-2 , 2-7; Part 3, pp. 3-6; Part 4, entire; Part 7, p. 6; Part 11, p. 2; Part 13, p. 2-4).

Second, and in some sense more important, Sayyid Imam indicates the circumstances under which these attacks became more likely (see, Sayyid Imam, "Exposure," Part 13, pp. 4-5), and they are directly related to al-Zawahiri's attempt to poison the reception of his "Rationalization," and therefore prevent the kind of genuine scholarly debate that Sayyid Imam believed was essential for restoring legality and pragmatics to the waging of jihad.

For the majority of a 10-hour, 2-day exclusive first-ever interview conducted in Turrah Prison, n.d., conducted just after release of "Rationalization," see *Al-Hayah*,"Egypt's Dr. Fadl of Al-Jihad Group Upbraids al-Qaeda's Al-Zawahiri," *Al-Hayah* in Arabic, Part One of a six-part interview with Al-Sayyid Imam Abd-al-Aziz al-Sharif: "Al-Hayah in Eguypt's Turrah Prison Interviews Author of the Document 'the Rationalization of Jihad in Egypt and the World'. Dr. Fadl: 'Al-Zawahiri Deceived me and was the Reason I was Accused in the Al-Sadat Case. I Left Jama'at al Jihad After it Insisted on Operations Inside Egypt and Distorted my

Book, 'A Compilation'," December 8, 2007, available from *www. opensource.com*; *Al-Hayah*, "Egypt: Former Al-Jihad Ideologue Rebukes 'Leaders Abroad', Al-Zawahiri," *Al-Hayah* in Arabic, Part Three of six-part interview with Al-Sayyid Imam Abd-al-Aziz al-Sharif: "*Al-Hayah* interviews the Author of the Document 'Rationalizing Jihad in Egypt and the World.' Dr. Fadl: al-Qaeda Does Not Have a Shari'a Scholar and Al-Zawahiri Turned Al-Jihad Members into Mercenaries," December 10, 2007, available from *www.opensource.com*; *Al-Hayah*,"Former Al-Jihad Theorist Says Document on Rationalization of Jihad Unaswerable," *Al-Hayah* in Arabic, Part Four of six-part interview with Al-Sayyid Imam Abd-al-Aziz al-Sharif: Al-Hayah Interviews Author of the Document "'Rationalizing Jihad in Egypt and the World." Dr. Fadl: Bin Ladin and Al-Zawahiri Are Creations of Intelligence Services and Were Playthings in the Hands of the Sudanese and Pakistanis," December 11, 2007, available from *www.opensource.com*; *Al-Hayah*, "Former Jihad Ideologue Attacks Bin Laden, Al-Zawahiri, 9/11 Atrocity," *Al Hayah* in Arabic, Part Six of six-part interview with Al-Sayyid Imam Abd-al-Aziz al-Sharif: "Al-Hayah in the Egyptian Turrah Prison interviews the author of 'The Rationalization of Jihad in Egypt and the World' document; Dr. Fadl: the victims of al-Qaeda through recruitment on the internet fill prisons purposelessly; my advice to Muslim youths: Learn your religion, learn your religion; and seek the truth," December 13, 2007, available from *www.opensource.com*.

For select examples of post-"Rationalization" responses, analyses, and commentary, see *Al-Misri al-Yawm*, "Al-Jihad organization leaders in the world voice support to Imam's revisions," *Al-Misri al-Yawm* in Arabic text of report by Ahmad al-Khatib headlined, "Al-Jihad leaders are anticipating Dr. Fadil's revisions, [Al-Jihad] world leaders support him," November 15, 2007, available from *www.opensource.gov*; *Nahdat Misr*, "'Rationalization of Jihad' Paper Triggers 'Crisis' Among Egyptian Fundamentalists," *Nahdat Misr* in Arabic: "Hani al-Siba'i: Rationalization of Jihad Document Product of Prisons, Lacks Credibility; Abu-Umar Al-Masri Responds: The Document is a Product of Sympathy, Mercy Not Coercion in Prison," November 20, 2007, available from *www. opensource.gov*; *Al-Misri Al-Yawm*, "Report on Reaction of Al-Jihad Revisions by Islamists Residing in London," Report by Ahmad Al-Khatib in *Al-Misri Al-Yawm* in Arabic : "Al-Misri al-Yawm opens the door for debate on Al-Jihad revisions," November 23, 2007, available from *www.opensource.gov*; Jihadist Websites, "Basir al-Tartusi Questions Shaykh Sayyid Imam's Words as Revisions, Retractions," Syrian Salafi cleric Abu-Basir al-Tartusi post to jihadist website, November 29, 2007, available from *www.opensource.gov*; *Al-Misri Al-Yawm*, "Egypt: Islamic Group Invites al-Qaeda to Commit to Sayyid Imam Revisions, Pins hope on Bin Laden," Report by Ahmad al-Khatib in *Al-Misri Al-Yawm* in Arabic: "The Islamic Group Demands Bin Laden and al-Zawahiri to Consider Sayyid Imam's Revisions 'Seriously'; In the first reaction, Karam Zuhdi and Najih Ibrahim: The document which Al-Misri Al-Yawm Published is unprecedented and its impact will reach al-Qaeda members," November 19, 2007, available from *www.opensource.gov*; MEMRI, "Major Jihadi Cleric and Author of Al-Qaeda's Shari'a Guide to Jihad: 9/11 Was a Sin; A Shari'a Court Should Be Set Up to Hold Bin Laden and Al-Zawahiri Accountable; There Are Only Two Kinds of People in Al Qaeda—The Ignorant and Those Who Seek Worldly Gain," MEMRI Special Dispatch Series No. 1785, December 14, 2007, available from *memri.org*; MEMRI, "Major Jihadi Cleric and Author of Al-Qaeda's Shari'a Guide to Jihad Sayyed Imam vs. Al Qaeda (2): Al-Zawahari Was Sudanese Agent—Sudan's VP Ali Othman Taha Hired Him to Attack Egypt; Ban on Jihad against Egyptian Regime in Egypt; Summary of Imam's New *Right Guidance for Jihad* Book," January 25, 2008, available from *memri.org*. For select Western analyses and commentary of this broader "revisionist" trend, see Jarret Brachman, "Al Qaeda's Dissident: How the Prison Writings of Sayyid Imam al-Sharif, One of al Qaeda's Founders Now Labeled a Turn Coat, are Doing More to Expose the Terrorist Group's Hypocrisy than Anyone Else," December 2009, available from *www.foreignpolicy.com*; Lawrence Wright, "The Rebellion Within: An Al Qaeda Mastermind Questions Terrorism," *The New Yorker*, June 2, 2008, pp. 37-53; Daniel Lav, "The Party of Jurisprudence vs. The Party of Action: Sayyed Imam, Ayman Al-Zawahiri, and the Split in the Jihad Movement," *MEMRI* Inquiry and Analysis Series, No. 144, May 29, 2008, available from *www.memri.org*; Omar Ashour, "Post-Jihadism and the Inevitability of Democratization," Arab Reform bulletin, November 10, 2009, available from *carnegieendowment.org/2009/11/10/post-jihadism-and-inevitability-of-democratization/kry*; Peter Bergen and Paul Cruickshank, "The Unraveling: Al Qaeda's Revolt Against Bin Laden," *The New Republic*, June 11, 2008; Nic Robertson and Paul Cruickshank, CNN, "New Jihad Code Threatens Al Qaeda," November 10, 2009, available from *edition.cnn.com/2009/WORLD/Africa/11/09/Libya.jihadi.code/*; Khalil Al-Anani, "Jihadi Revisionism: Will It Save The World?," Middle East Brief, No. 35, April 2009, pp. 1-7, available from *www. brandeis.edu/crown/publications/meb/MEB35.pdf*; IDC Herzliya, International Institute for Counter-Terrorism, "'Retracting' – Using Ideological Means for Purposes of De-Radicalization," January 2011, pp. 1-14, available from *www.ict.org.il/Portals/O/Internet%20 Monitoring%20Group/JWMG_Deradicalization.pdf.*

The Egyptian Islamic Group's (Al-Gama'a Al-Islamiyya) 1997 cessation of violence, and 2002/2003 revisionist writings, were unfortunately not available to this author in English translation. For select commentary on Al-Gama'a, see Y. Carmon, Y. Feldner, and D. Lav, "The Al-Gama'a Al-Islamiyya Cessation of Violence: An Ideological Reversal," *MEMRI Inquiry and Analysis Series*, No. 309, December 22, 2006, available from *memri.org*; Rudolph Peters, "The Notion of Jihad at the Turn of the 21st Century," in R. Peters, ed., *Jihad in Classical and Modern Islam: A Reader*, 2nd Ed., Princeton, NJ: Markus Wiener Publishers, esp. Chap. 3., "The Change of Strategy of the Egyptian Jama'a Islamiyya," pp. 180-183, for major revisions in jihad doctrine represented in the 2002/2003 books away from the notion of *kufr al-nizam* (the unbelief of the regime), and other doctrines; Omar Ashour, "Lions Tamed? An Inquiry into the Causes of De-Radicalization of Armed Islamist Movements: the Case of the Egyptian Islamic Group," *The Middle East Journal*, Vol. 61, No. 4, Autumn 2007, pp. 596+, available from *Academic OneFile, go.galegroup.com.*

34. The original article by Sheikh Salman al-Oudah, "Standing United Against Terrorism & al-Qaeda," was published September 21, 2009, available from *en.islamtoday.net/print/3490*. Apologizing for his "harsh words" and "harsh tone – which departs from my normal writing style – in order to confront those people who take up arms with the purpose of bringing death to numerous people and reducing societies to ruin," his teaser blurb states: "Today, I must stress how important it is to condemn the abominable and criminal acts being perpetrated around the world in Islam's name." See also his widely-quoted letter to Bin Laden: Shaykh Salman al-Oudah, "Shaykh Salman al-Oudah's Ramadan Letter to Osama bin Laden," September 18, 2007, available from *www. islamtoday.com/showme2.cfm?cat_id=29&sub_cat_id=1521.*

35. Sheikh Salman al-Oudah, "Standing United Against Terrorism & al-Qaeda," was published September 21, 2009, available from *en.islamtoday.net/print/3490*. "UPDATE: Standing United Against Terrorism & Al-Qaeda, Salman al-Oudah with Yasir Qa-

dhi, Yaser Birjas, Tawfique Chowdhurry, and Waleed Basyouni," March 10, 2009, available from *muslimatters.org/2009/10/12/sanding-united-against-terrorism-al-qaeda-salman-al-awdah-with-yasir-qadhi-and-yaser-birjas*.

36. *Ibid.*

37. *Ibid.*

38. *Ibid.*

39. Sheikh Salman al-Oudah, "Standing United Against Terrorism & al-Qaeda," September 21, 2009, available from *en.islamtoday.net/print/3490*.

40. *Al-Hayah*, "Former Jihad Ideologue Attacks Bin Laden, Al-Zawahiri, 9/11 Atrocity," *Al Hayah* in Arabic, Part Six of six-part interview with Al-Sayyid Imam Abd-al-Aziz al-Sharif: "Al-Hayah in the Egyptian Turrah Prison interviews the author of 'The Rationalization of Jihad in Egypt and the World'"; Dr. Fadl: the victims of al-Qaeda through recruitment on the internet fill prisons purposelessly; my advice to Muslim youths: Learn your religion, learn your religion; and seek the truth," December 13, 2007, available from *www.opensource.com*; See also, in his *Rationalizing Jihad, Part One*:

> The signatories to this document, in making known their dissatisfaction with those violations of shari'a and the corruption this caused, remind themselves and the general Muslims of some religious controls on the Fiqh [sic] theology of jihad. They affirm their commitment to these controls as mentioned in this document. They call on other Muslims, especially the young generations of Islam's youth, to be bound by them, and not to fall in the shari'a violations of their predecessors, as a result of ignorance of religion or deliberate action.

41. Al-Hakayimah is described by Sayyid Imam's interviewer, Muhammad Salah, as an "Egyptian fundamentalist" who is also a member of al-Qaeda.

42. Sayyid Imam, *Al-Hayah* Interview, Part Four; See also, additional mentions of the "overzealous attitudes and the phenomenon of young men joining organizations that exploit religion but do not faithfully follow religious teachings" in the same Part Four, *Al-Hayah* Interview. Sayyid Imam continues later, in his "Exposure": "I wanted to warn the people against them [al-Qaeda], especially Muslim youths whom they entrap through an array of deviate concepts and firebrand speeches in order to throw them in perils [sic] without any benefit and without the least achievement on the ground, except the media fanfare they use to cover up their crimes and confuse matters in the minds of people (Part 11, pp. 1-2); "I am mentioning this so that the budding generations of youth will be aware of how they were sold and gambled with, and so that no Muslim would venture to do something except with a fatwa from established ulemas. . . . So where is Al-Zawahiri from it [sic] as he incites with remote control?" (Part 11, p. 5); "I have written these words, as I have written 'The Document on Rationalizing Jihadist Action' ["Rationalization"] to warn Muslims, especially the young, against those opportunistic adventurers and their likes" (Part 12, p. 6).

43. According to Khalil Al-Anani, "Jihadi Revisionism: Will it Save the World?," No. 35, April 2009, available from *www.brandeis. edu/crown*, Sayyid Imam's major revisionist work represents "the most significant moment in jihadi revisionism" (p. 2), and that this is owing to Sayyid Imam's significance on three distinct fronts (p. 3): his biographical prestige owing to his actual proximity to 'jihadi' battlefields; his bibliographical prestige owing to his having provided in his two major 'pre-revisionist' works — *The Faithful Guide to Preparation* (*al-Umda fi 'idad al-idda*), a 500-plus work published in 1988 providing the "legal and operational parameters of jihadism"; and, *The Compendium in Pursuit of Divine Knowledge* (*al-Jami' fi talab al-'ilm al-sharif*), an 1,100-page work released in 1993; and third, the fact that Sayyid Imam's considered judgment has led to a substantial evolution in his explicit writings and interviews toward positions that fatally undercut the legal underpinnings of al-Qaeda's modus operandi. (See, esp.: Sayyid Imam Abd-al-Aziz al-Sharif, *Doctrine of Rationalization [i.e., Right Guidance] for Jihad Activity in Egypt and the World (Wathiqat Tarshid Al-'Aml Al-Jihadi fi Misr w'Al-Alam)*, November 2007, serialized in *Al-Sharq al-Awsat in Arabic*, available from *www.opensource.gov*.)

44. Owing to the highly-esteemed role of martyrdom "in the process of killing and being killed" in Islamic jurisprudence, history, and theology, and also its relative paucity as a tactic during the 1970s-90s, there is bare mention of this phenomenon and certainly not an extended objection on par with others raised. For recent scholarship examining the jurisprudential justifications and legal debates involved, see David Jan Slavicek, "Deconstructing the Shariatic Justification of Suicide Bombings," *Studies in Conflict and Terrorism*, Vol. 31, 2008, pp. 553-571; Shireen Khan Burki, "Haram or Halal? Islamists' Use of Suicide Attacks as 'Jihad'," *Terrorism and Political Violence*, Vol. 23, 2011, pp. 582-601. See also for a concise summary of a recently issued 600-page fatwa issued by Shaykh Muhammad Tahir-ul-Qadri: "Fatwa on Suicide Bombings and Terrorism: Table of Contents, Summary & Bibliography," Transl. Shaykh Abdul Aziz Dabbagh, Minhaj Publications, February 2010, available from *www.minhaj.org*.

45. See, for example, LIFG 2009, "Revisions," chs. 2, chs. 5; Sayyid Imam, "Rationalization," Part 1, pp. 2-3; 'Exposure,' Part 6, pp. 5-6; Part 13, pp. 6-7. Sayyid Imam, Al-Hayah interview, Part 3, virtually entirely calls into question the shari'a qualifications versus ignorance and worldly motives of Osama bin Laden and Ayman al-Zawahiri; Sayyid Imam, *Al-Hayah* Interview, Part 6, especially pp. 3-4. Sayyid Imam's assertion that al-Qaeda practices a "jurisprudence of justification" that privileges illicit ends and means, and then opportunistically gathers justificatory sources is particularly damning. See, for example, Sayyid Imam, "Rationalization," Part Two, esp. pp. 3-4; Sayyid Imam, Al-Hayah interview, Part 3, p. 7; Sayyid Imam, Al-Hayah Interview, Part 6, p. 4.

46. See especially LIFG 2009, "Revisions," ch. 6.

47. See especially *Ibid.*, ch. 4; Sayyid Imam, "Rationalization," Part 6, pp. 1-2.

48. See LIFG 2009, "Revisions," chs. 1, 9; Sayyid Imam, "Exposure," Part 2, pp. 2-4. This is also the major thrust of "The Amman Message," 2004. The latter is far more ecumenical than that proposed by jihad-realist salafi Sunni militants, however, in its willingness to embrace all extant schools of jurisprudence, including non-Sunni, non-salafi variants.

49. See LIFG 2009, ch. 4; Sayyid Imam, (see, "Rationalization," Part 6, p. 4), outlines and extensively treats the "six proscriptions each of which is sufficient on its own to spare the foreigners and tourists and not confront them with harm or damage." Having discussed them, he then asks rhetorically: "So how can the situation be when all these proscriptions or some of them are combined?" According to "Rationalization," Part 3, pp. 4-5, these proscriptions also apply to the financing of jihad:

> It is regrettable to see that some of those [for whom jihad has been waived because they do not have the expenses required]imposing on themselves a duty Allah has waived for them, and then resort to forbidden routes to collect money on the grounds of preparing for jihad. So they abduct innocent hostages to demand ransom, or rob the money of the ma'sumin [non-Muslims given a pledge of safety], and they might kill during the robbery of the people whose killing is not allowed. Aggression on the money and lives of the ma'sumin is a major sin, so those who commit it would have done something they are not allowed to do [aggressing on the lives of the ma'sumin] to perform a jihad that is not required of them by religion because of lack of money or other excuses. What theology is this? Nay, what mind is this? Is this not but a consequence of leadership by the ignorant and asking for their fatwas on issues of jihad? . . . [W]e tell all Muslims to desist from them, for the sinful acts of burglary and abductions and other forbidden acts cannot be sanctioned under the pretext of financing jihad.

See also, Sayyid Imam, "Exposure," Part 2, p. 4.

50. See, for example: Mohammad M. Hafez, "Chapter 2: Tactics, *Takfir*, and anti-Muslim Violence," in Assaf Moghadam and Brian Fishman, eds., *Self-Inflicted Wounds: Debates and Discussions within al-Qaeda and Its Periphery*, Harmony Project, Washington, DC: Combating Terrorism Center, December 16, 2010, p. 40: "[E]ven if certain actions are permissible in Islam, they should not be carried out without regard to the *circumstances* and *capabilities* of Muslims. Actions must be judged according to the balance between *masalih wa mafasid* (interests and harms). An action may be permissible in abstract,[sic] but when applied in practice it ceases

50

to be wise because its deleterious effects (*mafasid*) outweigh its presumed benefits (*masalih*)."

51. For example, Sayyid Imam lists the following options exercised by Prophet Muhammad as examples for those committed to upholding the shari'a but unable by ability of circumstance, to wage jihad: "These options ranged from disguise, hiding faith, going into seclusion, migration to Ethiopia and then Medina, pardon, forgiveness, and shunning the mushrikin [polytheistic idolaters], and the possibility of hurting the mushrikin by words, deeds, and patience on this, to jihad against the kuffar [infidels] including the mushrikin, apostates, and People of the Book [Christians and Jews] by sacrificing self and possessions by tongue, to the conclusion of truce and treaties." And he concludes in reference to contemporary duties to jihad: "There has been no change in any of these options, for all of them are legitimate according to the status of the establishment." Several additional examples of the relation of the duty to jihad in relation to actual capacities, and other options, are provided in this section.

52. See LIFG 2009, "Revisionism," Summary of experiences,' chs. 7, 8; Sayyid Imam, "Rationalization," Part 3, and especially Part 4.

53. See LIFG 2009, "Revisions," chs. 4, 8; Sayyid Imam, "Exposure," Part 3, p. 2.

54. See for example: *Qur'an* 4:43, 105-112; 16:126-127; 20:81-82; 35:45; 42:37, 40; 67:12-14.

55. See LIFG 2009, "Revisions," chs. 6, 8 for rather indirect inferences here; Sayyid Imam, "Rationalization," Part 7, pp. 3-4; Sayyid Imam, "Exposure," Part 2, p. 4; Part 4, pp. 4-6; Part 13, p. 5.

56. See especially Sayyid Imam, "Rationalization," Part 5 in general, and summary at p. 4-7. For the classical and still legally-compelling refutation of the underlying justification promulgated by violent takfiris responsible for Anwar Sadat's assassination, see Johannes J.G. Jansen, *The Neglected Duty: The Creed of Sadat's Assassins and Islamic Resurgence in the Middle East*, New York: Macmillan, 1986, pp. 54-62. In brief, the following points are the most salient: Only the denial of the Indivisibility and Sovereignty of

God disqualifies one as a Muslim (Qur'an 4:116); jihad includes, but significantly exceeds, martial fighting; put in its actual context, the charge that not ruling based on what God sent down amounts to unbelief, was actually addressed to the Jews, not the Muslims (Qur'an 5:48); Egypt by any reasonable standard observes Islamic dictates and where it does not, persons must remedy that to the last detail; there is no support in the Traditions for sanctifying let alone prescribing the violent removal of a leader who does perform the prayer ceremonies; the so-called sword verse (Qur'an 9:5) was directed at pagan polytheists, and is wholly inapplicable to observant Muslims; it is erroneous to equate the ruling regime in Egypt, whatever its faults, with the savage destruction meted out to Muslims by the Mongols (*Al-Tatar*); erroneous and opportunistic use of Ibn Taymiyyah's fatwas; referring to the *Faridah* as a "political pamphlet," errors are made regarding a de-contextualized and mythologized absolute oath of loyalty owed by an adherent to a ruling Caliph, in fact, and the Qur'an is largely silent on the precise means of selecting and holding accountable rulers of a Muslim political entity. Moreover, modern circumstances now empower the nation-state and its legitimate monopoly of violence to act on behalf of the citizenry in matters of war, justice, and peace; in contrast to a mystical praxis jihad doctrine, Islamic jurisprudence upholds the necessity of deep knowledge in Islam, and of the world and its circumstances: this is also a means of "striving and struggling in the path of Allah" or jihad; there is great historical precedent for Muslim cooperation with non-Muslims; the author of the *Faridah* is merely a contemporary exponent of a specific deviant movement within Islam — the khawarij, or "Kharijis," whose fanaticism, self-righteous arrogance, and violent willingness to takfir virtually all who disagree; and finally, in stark contrast to the claim that jihad is a "nonfulfilled duty," he states:

> Qur'an and Sunnah, so the Mufti teaches, command Muslims to resist the enemies of Islam, but they certainly do not order attacks on other Muslims, or on non-Muslim compatriots. Jews and Christians must have freedom of cult and belief, the Mufti insists. They have the same rights as Muslim citizens, he continues. The character of jihad, so we must understand, has now changed radically, because the defense of the country and religion is nowadays the duty of the regular army, and this army

carries out the collective duty of jihad on behalf of all citizens. 'To conquer oneself and Satan' is equally part of the Muslim duty of jihad, the Mufti adds, while calling other Muslims apostates is not. Whatever the people of the *Faridah* and their sympathizers might say, jihad is, according to the Mufti, not a forgotten or absent duty at all (p. 60).

57. Jihad-realist jurisprudential objections—the focus of the above—are also complemented by a vast literature comprising resolutions, Fatawa, letters, and official rulings, which together reinforce many salient points raised above regarding the sinful and illegal acts perpetrated by the terrorist enterprise. See, for example: *The Amman Declaration*: King Abdullah II bin Al-Hussein of Jordan, (The Hashemite Kingdom of Jordan), "The Amman Message," November 9, 2004, available from *ammanmessage.com*. (Now includes "The Official Website of THE AMMAN MESSAGE," available from *ammanmessage.com*, launched, March 1, 2007); International Islamic *Fiqh* Academy, "The Three Points of the Amman Message, V. 2," June 2006, available from *ammanmessage.com*; The Mardin *Conference:* Reuters, "Islam Scholars Recast Jihadists' Favorite Fatwa: Declaration is Latest Bid to Counter Militant Islam," March 31, 2010, available from *www.alarabiya.net/save_print.php?print=1&cont_id=104563&lang=en*; Muslim World League, "Document: What is Jihad? What is Terrorism? Statement by Muslim Scholars,"available from *www.middle-east-online.com/English/?cat=main&page=1&id=174*; Charles Kurzman, "Islamic Statements Against Terrorism," available from *kurzman.unc.edu/Islamic-statements-against-terrorism/* (Updated November 16, 2010); Council on American-Islamic Relations (CAIR), "CAIR's Anti-Terrorism Campaigns," available from *www.cair.com/americanmuslims/antiterrorism.aspx*; Sheila Musaji, "Muslim Voices Against Extremism and Terrorism– Part 1 – Fatwas and Formal Statements by Muslim Scholars & Organizations – updated," January 28, 2011, available from *www.theamericanmuslim.org;*

58. This term "Lord Christ" is very likely a mistranslation from the original Arabic text since Muslims, though regarding Jesus (Isa) as an immaculately conceived Prophet who revealed the Gospel, deny both the lordship and messiahship implied in each of those titles.

59. Sayyid Imam Abd-al-Aziz al-Sharif, *Doctrine of Rationalization [i.e., Right Guidance] for Jihad Activity in Egypt and the World (Wathiqat Tarshid Al-'Aml Al-Jihadi fi Misr w'Al-Alam)*, November 2007, serialized in *Al-Sharq al-Awsat* in Arabic, available from *www.opensource.gov*. Also, *Ibid.* "In the domain of jihad for the sake of Allah the Almighty, this is one of the branches of faith, or 'the peak of Islam's hump', as correctly cited from the beloved chosen one [Muhammad], Allah's prayers and peace upon him."

60. LIFG 2009, "Revisions," ch. 4; Sayyid Imam, "Rationalization" Part 1, p. 2; and especially Part 6 (entire). Though it may strike non-Muslims as immoral, a key ground for not targeting persons based on nationality includes the possibility that Muslims themselves will be harmed: for example, Sayyid Imam, "Rationalization," Part 6, examines six proscriptions against killing non-Muslims and begins the list with the possibility that a Muslim may be among them. Also, "Rationalization," Part 7, deals again with the unlawfulness of conducting bombings in non-Muslim countries by first stating that Muslims themselves may be killed (p. 1-2; again at pp. 4-5).

61. LIFG 2009, "Revisions," ch. 4; Sayyid Imam,'Rationalization' Part 1, p. 2; and especially Part 6 (entire); Sayyid Imam, "Exposure," Part 4, p. 3; Part 6, p. 5.

62. Sayyid Imam, "Rationalization," Part 5, p. 3; Part 7, extensively discussed at pp. 2, 4-5; Sayyid Imam, "Exposure," Part 2, p. 4; Part 4, p. 4.

63. LIFG 2009, ch. 4; Sayyid Imam, "Rationalization," Part 1, p. 2; Sayyid Imam, 'Rationalization' Part 5, p. 3; On p. 6, he states: "The alternative is not killing civilians, foreigners, tourists, destroying property, or aggression on the blood and property of the ma'sumin [inviolable] under the claims of jihad. All this is *haram*"; Sayyid Imam, "Rationalization," Part 7, pp. 3-4; Sayyid Imam, *Al-Hayah* interview, Part 4, p. 3; On p. 5, Sayyid Imam goes so far as to say:

> I say this to those who defend al-Qaeda's leaders: Your friends Bin Ladin and Al-Zawahiri and their followers are treacherous, backstabbing people. God, may He be

praised, forbade you to act as advocate for such persons. Anyone who admires their deeds is a partner in sin. They are now counted as people of weak faith because they have committed the major sins of lying and treachery. Only a thin line separates them from being outright infidels. The ancient Muslims said that "major sins are the path to disbelief." These sins are the introduction to disbelief. God Almighty said: "In the long run evil in the extreme will be the end of those who do evil because they rejected the Signs of God, and held them up to ridicule" [Qur'an 30:10].

See also Sayyid Imam, *Al-Hayah* interview, Part 6, p. 2: "It is inadmissible for a Muslim to betray the trust of the people of the country in their blood, honor, or funds, or act treacherously against them in the name of jihad. So the 9/11 attacks were wrong and contradicted the Islamic shari'a."; Sayyid Imam, "Exposure," Part 1, p. 3; Part 2, p. 4; Part 5, entire; Part 6, pp. 1-2, 4-6; Part 13, p. 5; See also, *Al Misri Al-Yawm* in Arabic, "Jihad Mufti Condemns 09/11 Bombings, Opposes Building Mosque Near Ground Zero," September 18, 2010, available from *www.opensource.gov*.

64. See, for example, Sayyid Imam, "Rationalization," Part 6, p. 4:

We believe that it is by no means permissible to assume the right to kill a human being just because he belongs to a certain country [killing on nationality]. This heterodoxy is without precedent in the heritage of the [Muslim] Nation. Affiliation by an individual to a certain country is no proof of his Islam or kufr, for the objective of affiliation to nations and similar affiliations is just identification. . . . So killing on nationality is a hideous heterodoxy without precedent in the heritage of the Nation.

See also Sayyid Imam, *Al-Hayah* interview, Part 3, p. 7:

[Salah] Some organizations have denied that there are groups that select and kill their victims on the basis of nationality. They claim that they carry out these operations in the context of their war against the West and the Arab regimes. [Al-Sharif] This is not true. al-Qaeda and Bin Ladin announced more than once that they target U.S.

citizens without discrimination. This is what they did on 9/11. They killed on the basis of nationality. Groups that sympathized with them carried out the Madrid bombings in 2004, killing Spaniards indiscriminately. In the London Underground bombings in 2005, they killed British citizens on the basis of nationality. All this was killing on the basis of nationality. Being a citizen of a particular country is not proof of disbelief or faith. It is not evidence of declaring the lives of certain persons forfeit or that their property is forfeit.

See Sayyid Imam, "Exposure," Part 2, p. 4; Part 4, pp. 2-3.

65. Sayyid Imam, "Rationalization," Part 1, pp. 4-5:

In this great domain, the domain of jihad, the slavery of the Muslim to his God the Almighty is [sic] by giving precedence to his God's quest from him over his own quest for himself. . . . This is done through the Muslim knowing what Allah has made a duty for him at a certain time, according to his ability. He gets reward for what he is able to do, and he is absolved from the sin of what he could not do. This is the way of the Muslims in all affairs, on jihad and other issues. . . . [F]or the Muslim to place an objective for himself that is beyond his capacity and not suitable to his conditions, even if it is legitimate in itself, and then follow any road to attain his objective, without being bound by the restrictions of Shari'a, then would have given precedence to his quest from himself over his God's quest from him. This is not the way of the Muslims but the way of the revolutionary secularists. In Islam, there is no such thing as 'the end justifies the means', [sic] even if the end is noble and legitimate to begin with. On the contrary, a Muslim worships Allah through the means used just as he worships Him through the ends sought. If he dies before getting his end, he gets the reward for trying, and he is absolved from the sin of what he could not do.

In Sayyid Imam, "Rationalization," Part 4, this is also extensively discussed; see also, Sayyid Imam, "Exposure," Part 2, p. 3; Part 3, pp. 2-3.

66. See LIFG 2009, "Revisions," ch. 4; Sayyid Imam, "Rationalization," Part 4, p. pp. 1-2; Sayyid Imam, "Exposure," Part 2, pp. 3-4; Part 3, pp. 3-5; Part 10, p. 3.

67. See Sayyid Imam, *Al Hayah* interview, Part 1, p. 5.

68. *Ibid.*, Part 6, p. 2. Since the law of jihad rules that a "powerless person in infidel countries is not required to conduct jihad" other options must be exercised, including: "engage in a jihad that propagates the Islamic call," and "[i]f they are unable to do that, they can repudiate abominable acts in their hearts, which is a duty in any case," or he "can conceal his faith and use what is allowed in the shar'iah, like dissimulation." This key question faced by Muslims living in non-Muslim majority societies led to virtually an identical response from the salafi "jihadist" cleric Mohammad Tahir al-Barqawi (aka Shaykh Abu-Muhammad al-Maqdisi), i.e., he encourages several nonviolent alternatives for promoting the Islamic call in Belgium, empowering and protecting the Muslim Umma, and also, interacting on the basis of reciprocity and fairness with those who do the same. See Jihadist websites, "Al-Maqdisi Advises Muslims in Belgium on How to Deal with Non-Muslim Society," April 23, 2010, available from *www.opensource.com*.

69. See Sayyid Imam, *Al-Hayah* Interview, Part 6, p. 2:

> If an enemy invades a Muslim land jihad against the enemy is an individual duty. If Muslims are unable to take on jihad, it becomes the duty of neighboring Muslim countries, if they are capable of conducting jihad. In case they are incapable, Muslims are duty bound to leave the country. . . . Whoever is incapable of jihad or emigration, may stay in the country and make a truce with the enemy without committing sins or harming other Muslims. In short, the options are either take on jihad, emigrate, or conclude a truce.

See also, Sayyid Imam, "Exposure," Part 2, p. 3; Part 3, pp. 2-3; Part 9, pp. 1-3.

70. See Sayyid Imam, *Al-Hayah* Interview, Part 6, p. 3:

The issue of killing civilians of the subjects of countries occupying Muslim countries is explained in the document ['Rationalization']. The gist is that whoever enters enemy countries on a visa, even if forged, must not act treacherously against the people of that country, betray their trust, kill them, or steal their money. It is not admissible to kill civilians or combatants. Ulema do not disagree over this issue.

See also, Sayyid Imam, "Exposure," Part 6, pp. 3-4; Part 10, p. 5; Part 13, p. 5.

71. See LIFG 2009, "Revisions," chs. 7, 8; Sayyid Imam, "Exposure," Part 3, p. 1; Part 10, p. 2, 5; Part 12, p. 2, 3. The linkage between the law, and pragmatics, is clearly stated by Sayyid Imam in "Exposure," Part 10, p. 5:

[W]hat then would you say about Bin Laden and Al-Zawahiri and their followers who betrayed the Emir [violation of bay'at], hit their enemy in the back [violation of security pact, visa], and brought catastrophes to the Muslims [pragmatics] destroying groups and States and filling graveyards and prisons with Muslims, in addition to founding a criminal doctrine to justify wholesale killing . . . So what do you say to these people? I leave it to the Muslims to judge them. A debauched person who drinks liquor hurts no one but himself. But the damage of those [sic] we refer to is wholesale.

And again, Sayyid Imam provides this linkage in Sayyid Imam, "Exposure," Part 13, p. 2:

So Muslim folks do not be deceived by any body [sic] who talks about religion and jihad until you judge him by Shari'a. . . . So how about those who bring disasters to the Muslims, destroy States and groups, adulterate religion and replace it with heresies and inaccuracies that are counter to Allah's Book, and also cause the killing and imprisonment of tens of thousands of Muslims? How are they to be described? What good is it to demolish two buildings in the United States and it [the US] demolishes the Taliban State, the only State in the world that welcomed fugitive Muslims? Bin Ladin then fled and left the Afghans to pay the price for his foolhardiness in death, homelessness, and large-scale ruin. He sheds tears for the children of Palestine and forgets the children of Afghanistan whose blood is spilled every day because of him. . . .

See also, Sayyid Imam, in *Al Misri Al-Yawm* in Arabic, "Jihad Mufti Condemns 09/11 Bombings, Opposes Building Mosque Near Ground Zero," September 18, 2010, available from *www. opensource.gov.*

72. The Israel-Palestine conflict was significantly underplayed in the The *9/11 Commission Report*, and according to the follow-up volume describing the Commission's inside-story, this was the result of a compromise. Thomas A. Kean and Lee H. Hamilton, *Without Precedent: The Inside Story of the 9/11 Commission*, New York: Alfred A. Knopf, 2006, p. 284-285:

We did, however, have some disagreement over foreign policy issues. Much of it revolved around the question of Al Qaeda's motivation. For instance, Lee felt that there had to be an acknowledgment that a settlement of the Israeli-Palestinian conflict was vital to America's long-term relationship with the Islamic world, and that the presence of American forces in the Middle East was a major motivating factor in al Qaeda's actions. . . . This was sensitive ground. Commissioners who argued that al Qaeda was motivated primarily by religious ideology—and not by opposition to American policies—rejected mentioning the Israeli-Palestinian conflict in the report. In their view, listing U.S. support for Israel as a root cause of Al Qaeda's opposition to the United States indicated that the United States should reassess that policy. To Lee, though, it was not a question of altering support for Israel but of merely stating a fact that the Israeli-Palestinian conflict was central to the relations between the Islamic world and the United States—and to Bin Ladin's ideology and the support he gained throughout the Islamic world for his jihad against America.

Moreover, the *9/11 Commission Report* does acknowledge, at least with respect to Khalid Sheik Muhammad (KSM), this motivation: " [Ramzi] Yousef's instant notoriety as the mastermind of the 1993 World Trade Center bombing inspired KSM to become involved in planning attacks against the United States. By his own account, KSM's animus toward the United States stemmed not from his experiences there as a student, but rather from his violent disagreement with U.S. foreign policy favoring Israel. (Source: *The 9/11 Commission Report*, New York: W.W. Norton, 2004, p. 147.

Ramzi Yousef, mastermind of the 1993 World Trade Center plot, as well as others, including the initial planning of the "Planes Operation" — who had earlier failed in an attempt to bomb the Israeli embassy in Bangkok, Thailand, and whose initial New York targets were not the World Trade Center but targeting Jewish neighborhoods in Crown Heights and Williamsburg — had this to say as a final statement following his conviction for that crime:

We are, the fifth battalion in the Liberation Army, declare our responsibility for the explosion on the mentioned building. This action was done in response for the American political, economical and military support to Israel the state of terrorism and to the rest of the dictator countries in the region.

Our demands:
Stop all military, economical, and political aids [sic] to Israel.
All diplomatic relations with Israel must stop.
Not to interfere with any of the Middle East countries [sic] interior affairs.

... The terrorism that Israel practices (which is supported by America) must be faced with a similar one. The dictatorship and terrorism (also supported by America) that some countries are practicing against their own people must also be faced with terrorism.

The American people must know, that their civilians who got killed are not better than those who are getting killed by the American weapons and support.

The American people are responsible for the actions of their government and they must question all of the crimes that their government is committing against other people. Or they – Americans – will be the targets of our operations that could diminish them.

We invite all of the people from all countries and all of the revolutionaries in the world to participate in this action with us to accomplish our just goals.

"IF THEN ANYONE TRANSGRESSES THE PROHIBITION AGAINST YOU TRANSGRESS YE LIKEWISE AGAINST HIM . . .

AL-FARBEK AL-ROKN, Abu Bakr Al-Makee (Simon Reeve, *The New Jackals: Ramzi Yousef, Osama bin Laden, and the Future of Terrorism*, Boston, MA: Northeastern University Press, 1999, "Appendix Three: A letter from Ramzi Yousef and the other conspirators in the World Trade Center bombing, published as received by the New York Times four days after the February 1993 explosion," pp. 274-275.)

CNN in its write-up of the final verdict represented facts in the following manner: "After three days of deliberation in November, a federal jury convicted Yousef and Eyad Ismoil on murder and conspiracy charges for their roles in a plot by Islamic extremists to topple the trade centers two 110story [sic] towers to punish the United States for its support of Israel," available from *articles. cnn.com/1998-01-08/us/9801 08 yousef 1 trade-center-bombing-yousef-and-eyad-ismoil-conviction-S=PM:US.* For a chillingly-prescient, sympathetic account of Yousef's motives, but not tactics, see Jude Wanniski, "The mind of a terrorist" September 12, 2001, available from *www.wnd.com/index.php?pageId=10813.*

Finally, at least one of the East Africa Embassy bombers made his motives known in published transcripts of the case (See *United States of America v. Osama bin Laden et al.,* S(7) 98 Cr. 1023, United States District Court, Southern District of New York, New York, October 18, 2001, Sentencing hearing), available from *fl1.findlaw. com/news/findlaw.com/cnn/docs/binladen/usbinldn101801.pdf.*

El-Hage's complicity in the attacks was proved, but based on his testimony one learns that policy, not shari'a, primarily motivated him; also, that the killing of innocent human beings — something he apparently did not know would happen — is absolutely unacceptable under Islamic law. The defendants Wadih El Hage, Mohamed Sadeek Odeh, Mohamed Rashed Daoud Al-'Owhali, and Khalfan Khamis Mohamed all received life without parole: Odeh's views (see p. 112) are referred to by Judge Leonard B. Sand when he states as motives, Mr. Odeh's opposition to United States' support of Israel, financially, politically and militarily, [and] presence of the "United States military in the holy lands of Saudi Arabia, [and] the Persian Gulf and the Horn of Africa." At p. 113, Judge Sands states: "The attack may have been intended to attack American foreign policy, but the victims were innocent people. . . ." At pages 115-116, the distinction is made between support of al-Qaeda's military goals and deep regret at loss of innocent civilian life. His attorney, Anthony L. Ricco, states:

> He is now prepared to face the sentence that the court must impose here. He is very much aware of the substantial human loss that occurred here. He is not oblivious to the fact that many people were injured and many people died here who were innocent. He acknowledged that very early on in the case when he was interrogated. He has always expressed that. He does not have remorse, your Honor, about his participation in Al Qaeda. That's a difference in his mind. . . . Mohamed Odeh has always stated that he was not a part of the execution of the bombing. He continues in that position today, but that does not mean, your Honor, that he is a person who is oblivious to the great loss of human life and the great injury that was inflicted upon people here (pp. 115-116).

El-Hage, a second defendant, addressed the Court before his sentencing with a very revealing, fundamentalist narrative but one that appears to recognize the enormity of killing innocents and indeed one that exhibits moral revulsion. His view of the United States is positive from a Muslim perspective: he repeatedly refers to the U.S. as a land where Islam can be freely spread and practiced ("Others chose to migrate to other countries, such as the U.S., where they can spread the message of Islam freely and in the same time support their brothers and sisters who are continuing their efforts to apply God's rules in the Islamic countries," p. 139); also: "Islam became the fastest growing religion in the U.S., as it is in the whole world, all praise be to God first, and to the tolerant, open society here," (p. 139); also: "Now, even though the Islamic system and way of life is for the best of all humanity [sic], devout Muslims, as I believe, are not asking to apply it here in the U.S., where Muslims are less than 7 million. They are a minority. The fact is that they want to apply it in the Islamic countries where the majority are Muslims. But in those countries, today's selfish, arrogant and self-deceited kings, presidents and rulers want to apply their own self-invented rules . . . [T]o make the long story short [sic], by the 20th century, the rulers started to neglect the Koranic laws, substituting them with manmade [sic] laws. The result is what we see today. Muslim nations are the weakest, poorest and most miserable. That is why, in my opinion, we find devout, committed Muslims, individuals and groups, working actively to re-implement God's rules and guidance" (pp. 137-138).

As for moral revulsion: "[D]evout Muslims, . . . even in time of conflict, they should not exceed certain limits, harming innocent people or noncombatant ones. This is very stressed upon [sic] in the Koran and the teachings of the prophet Muhammad, peace be upon him, who even prohibited destroying crops, animals or property at time of war (p. 139); and again:

> When the bombings happened in Africa in '98, my opinion was that that action was extreme and not in accordance with the beliefs that I learned. I made my opinion clear well before I was arrested or charged. Today, my opinion is still the same towards what happened in Africa and what happened here last month [9/11]. The killing of innocent people and noncombatant is radical, extreme and cannot be tolerated by any religion, principles, beliefs or values. Today I can stand here and say that I did not participate or support any extreme conduct or any act that violates my beliefs as a devout Muslim. . . (pp. 141-142).

El-Hage at pp. 142-143 identifies "many American policies towards Muslim countries [that] are wrong" including the alleged "over one million child [sic] and thousands of innocent people" affected by the embargo on Iraq; "the unconditional support of the American government to the Israeli government that is killing innocent Palestinians, taking their land, expelling them and destroying their homes" (p. 142); the effect on deeply religious Muslims of "having non-Muslim troops on the land of Muslims' holiest sites, its negative impact on Muslim masses around the world and specifically those on the Arabian Peninsula" (p. 142). He goes on to also say though: "Such policies, in my opinion, are wrong and end up breeding unjustified extremism. . . . Many Muslims and non-Muslims have expressed the same views. That includes the American Muslim community, which I am a member of, which is free to voice its criticism to the American policy [sic] but without committing or supporting any extreme acts" (pp. 142-143). And in his defense he also states: "I am still the person who avoids radical solutions and acts, as I did in the past" (p. 145). [El-Hage had at that time no prior record of any violent or illegal activity.]

Bin Laden's butchery and contrast with El-Hage could not be greater. He acknowledges El-Hage: "[He] was one of our brothers whom God was kind enough to steer to the path of relief work for Afghan refugees. I still remember him, though I have not seen him or heard from him for many years. He has nothing to do with the U.S. allegations" (*FBIS Report*, January 2004, "Time Magazine Interview with Bin Laden," January 11, 1999, pp. 83-86). In stark contrast to El-Hage's revulsion, Bin Laden answers the *TIME* magazine correspondent's question, "[H]ow can you justify the death of Africans?" (p. 84), by invoking the 'jihad of justification' and extends the *Tartarrus* (human shield) doctrine to justify the mass murder in Nairobi, Kenya, on August 7, 1998, of 213 persons, and injuring of 4500; and in Dar as Salam (literally, "House of Peace"), Tanzania, to 11 dead, and 85 injured." (See *United States of America v. Osama bin Laden et al.*, S(7) 98 Cr. 1023, United States District Court, Southern District of New York, New York, N.Y., March 12, 2001, Superseding Indictment, pp. 43-44, available from *www.haguejusticeportal.net/Docs/NLP/US/US_v_Osama_bin_Laden_et_al_Superseding Indictment-1.pdf ; 2.pdf; 3.pdf.*) See, finally, Fawaz A. Gerges, *America and Political Islam: Clash of Cultures or Clash of Interests*, New York: Cambridge University Press, 1999, esp. pp. 238-242, for several prescient suggestions the actual implementation of which may have substantially altered the events defining the decade to come.